DISCARDED

DISCARDED

LIBERTY AND DESPOTISM
IN SPANISH AMERICA

LIBERTY AND DESPOTISM IN SPANISH AMERICA

BY
CECIL JANE

WITH A PREFACE BY
SALVADOR DE MADARIAGA
King Alfonso XIII Professor of Spanish Studies in
the University of Oxford

COOPER SQUARE PUBLISHERS, INC.
NEW YORK
1966

980.03
J33l

109017

First published by The Oxford University Press
At The Clarendon Press
Reprinted by arrangement with The Oxford University Press

Published 1966 by
Cooper Square Publishers, Inc.
59 Fourth Avenue, New York, N. Y. 10003
Library of Congress Catalog Card Number: 66-29053

PRINTED IN THE UNITED STATES OF AMERICA
by SENTRY PRESS, NEW YORK, N. Y. 10019

PREFACE

THAT the first book to be published by the Oxford University Press under the auspices of the Chair of Spanish Studies at Oxford should be one on a Spanish-American subject will be readily understood. The Chair was deliberately described ' of Spanish studies ' because it was felt that it should become a centre for the development and encouragement of all the intellectual activities connected with Spanish civilization in general. The subject of this book will emphasize the world-wide nature of the civilization born of Spain.

It is a civilization which has not always met with all the sympathy and understanding which it deserves. Ignorance and prejudice have woven round the history of the Spanish Empire a thick veil through which the simplest and most obvious facts are, more than distorted, actually invisible, so that when the veil is torn aside by a friendly hand the facts appear so unfamiliar as to be at times unbelievable.

If such misunderstandings obtain when the facts are fairly simple and straightforward, what can we expect when history is but a bewildering sequence of violent movements, revolutions, wars, cessions, dictatorships, such as the lives of the Spanish-American Republics have often presented to the inattentive glance of the distant observer. Puzzled and irritated by this seemingly chaotic agitation, the foreign observer usually gave up all attempt at understanding the position, and took a comfortable refuge in the scanty but safe generalities which he had heard at school. Then the blessed word ' backward ' covered absence of thought with the absence of meaning which it conveys in the hollow of its neat shape.

And yet—at any rate for the English-speaking world—the countries born of the Iberian nations are of primary interest. Great Britain is clearly united to many of them by ties of trade and political tradition; the United States of America has felt a kind of continental fraternity with them ever since they broke away from Spain. Such natural elements of good relationship and co-operation should not be hampered by the lack of sympathy which an insufficient or defective knowledge is bound to breed. The political instability of the Spanish-American Republics has been a permanent source of moral and material weakness to them. Apart from the political evils which it has entailed in their home life, it has jeopardized their reputation abroad to such an extent that foreign observers have not even troubled to inquire whether there was a reasonable explanation for it.

Mr. Cecil Jane must be congratulated for having wondered whether, after all, there was not such a cause— and an honourable cause at that—which could explain that a whole continent should have to struggle amongst powerful inner and outer difficulties towards a definite and stable political constitution. He has approached his subject by the best possible avenue. There was a time when politics were supposed to be but disguised economics. We think nowadays that both politics and economics are but manifestations of psychology, and Mr. Jane has boldly and clearly built on this view his interpretation of Spanish-American political evolution. His work rises therefore on solid ground. And since he speaks as an Englishman to Englishmen and Americans, he may hope to succeed, where a less impartial advocate might have failed, in performing the great service of interpreting to one another the two great European civilizations which stand at the basis of whatever the future reserves for the great continent of America.

S. DE M.

NOTE

THE employment of any single term to denominate all those states which have replaced the former Spanish Empire on the mainland of the American continent may appear to ignore the fact that between the peoples of those states great differences exist. Those differences, the inevitable result of variations in natural conditions, tend continually to increase as a result of immigration from the Old World and of the fact that development proceeds more rapidly in some states than it proceeds in others. But the use of a single descriptive term is none the less wholly legitimate. The differences are rather superficial than fundamental. Despite their existence, the republics are still bound together by community of language, creed, and tradition; they share one cultural heritage and one historic past. The ' Fiesta de la Raza ' is no idle ceremony. It is an expression of that deep spiritual unity, transcending all minor differences, which links together all the nations of the Spanish-speaking world.

C. J.

96 ALEXANDRA ROAD,
  LONDON, N.W. 8.
    August 1929.

CONTENTS

I

THE POLITICAL CHARACTER OF THE REPUBLICS

THE political life of all those states which during the early years of the last century arose upon the ruins of the Spanish Empire on the American mainland presents two common features. In all those states, constitutions of the most liberal and democratic character have been promulgated; in all, there have from time to time arisen dictators whose absolute power has been either frankly proclaimed or thinly veiled under constitutional forms. So frequently has such personal rule been established in many of the states that in them there has appeared to be an almost perpetual and complete contradiction between theory and practice, between the nominal and the actual systems of government.

On the one hand it has been everywhere declared that the basis of state organization must be found in those conceptions of individual and collective freedom which inspired the theorists of the French Revolution or which have received practical recognition in England. The dogma that legitimate political power can be derived only from the will of the people has been explicitly proclaimed; the right of the citizens to change their form of government at any time has been expressly admitted. In every state, republics, representative and democratic, have been created; in two states only has any other form of organization been even contemplated, in one only, Mexico, adopted even momentarily. Titles of honour have been universally abolished; the absolute equality of all citizens before the law has been recognized. Those rights which may be deemed essential for the enjoyment of personal liberty have been guaranteed to all residents in the republics; to the citizens have been secured all those privileges which must be accorded to members of a democratic state. Definite clauses in the constitutions have established freedom of speech, freedom of the press, freedom of association for all legitimate purposes, freedom to hold and to express any political opinions. To all has been granted the right to move at will from place to place and to engage in any lawful occupation. Speedy and even justice, and exemption from arbitrary punishment and from arbitrary exactions, have been declared to be the due of all; the personal liberty of no one is to be abridged save by just process of law. Complete religious toleration has been proclaimed; free and secular education expressly provided. Local interests have been equally safeguarded; in three of the republics, the Argentine, Mexico, and Venezuela, a federal organization has been adopted in order that the special conditions and needs of particular districts may be better considered. Everywhere, in short, a régime of the most complete liberty compatible with security for life, limb and property, and with the continued existence of the state, has been established, so far as such a result can be attained by the medium of a written constitution.

On the other hand in every one of the republics a very different régime has at times actually existed. In some cases, power has been openly seized by individuals who have suspended or abrogated the constitution and who have frankly asserted their own despotic authority. In other cases a similar situation has been produced by less direct and open methods. There appears in all the constitutions an emergency clause permitting the executive in times of crisis to assume discretionary powers. This clause has been invoked, while the provision contained in it, that the duration of the exercise of such powers should be strictly limited to the duration of the crisis, has been disregarded. A perpetual 'state of siege' has been created, a condition not contemplated by the constitution which has been professedly observed. But whether an open or a veiled dictatorship has been established the result has been the same; in either case, the guarantees of liberty have ceased to be operative. The press has been shackled; freedom of speech and freedom of political association have been denied. Justice has been subordinated to the interest of the executive, and arbitrary punishments for political offences have been inflicted. Severe restraints have been imposed upon the private activities of citizens; religious toleration has in many cases ceased to exist, and the liberty of individuals, of communities, of the nation as a whole, has been so impaired as to be practically destroyed by a system which has been based, not upon the suffrages of an electorate, but upon the possession of an armed force.

To a very great extent the political history of the republics has been a record of alternating periods of liberty and despotism. In all these states there has been a more or less continuous struggle between two methods of government. At times that struggle has been conducted peacefully; its existence has been more real than apparent. At other times it has assumed a violent character. Some states have been the scene of revolution after revolution until their normal condition has seemed to be one of anarchy tempered by interludes of despotism. To the unthinking or to the ill-informed the Spanish American republics have, indeed, become something of a byword. In Europe it has often been alleged or suggested that they are perpetually disturbed. They have been depicted as presenting an unhappy spectacle of communities attempting to govern themselves and failing lamentably in that attempt, as being lands in which there is no adequate security for life, limb or property, as the very heaven of unscrupulous political adventurers. It has been hastily assumed that their political condition is so obvious as not to require any careful investigation, that it offers no features meriting consideration, that the vicissitudes through which the republics have passed and are passing can in no sense be regarded as the outcome of any conflict of principles or of ideals.

Such failure to devote any real consideration to the political history of the republics has resulted in a misconception both of the nature and the origin of that conflict of which they have been and are the scene. By very many this conflict has been dismissed somewhat contemptuously. It has been easily explained as the outcome of personal ambitions and of personal rivalries, as a struggle in which the protagonists are actuated by no other motive than a desire for self-aggrandizement, and their respective supporters by nothing save a desire for booty. It has been assumed that those who have attained power have been mere adventurers availing themselves of the incurable corruption of their states to secure their own advancement. Those who have opposed the actual holders of power have been regarded as no more honourable or reputable. Their opposition has been put down to envy, jealousy, disappointed ambition. The political life of the republics has thus been reduced to nothing more than the sordid bickerings of greedy knaves and selfish cliques, whose sole desire is to attain a position which may enable them to plunder the rest of the community. The result of such strife matters little. It is certain that, in any event, the conduct of the holders of power will be equally corrupt, equally devoid of principle or patriotism; in any event, it is by rogues that the government will be controlled.

This conception of the conflict, however, is intrinsically improbable and is perhaps demonstrably false. It may be admitted that in producing the particular type of political life which prevails in the republics, personal ambition has played and probably will always play a part. Very many of these states present an almost unique field for adventure of every kind. For the explorer there are thousands of square miles of unknown territory; for the anthropologist and the archeologist wonderful remains of bygone civilization lie hidden in the depths of tropical forests and they may find untamed and unspoiled native tribes wandering through districts which have, perhaps, never yet been trodden by the foot of civilized man. There is no less scope for the adventurer of commerce or finance. Large areas are still wholly undeveloped, vast resources still untapped; there alone in modern times can tales of hidden treasure assume an aspect of probability.

There are as unique opportunities for the adventurer of politics. Great prizes seem to await the daring. The careers of such men as Billinghurst appear to prove that no height is unattainable by the man of bright courage and firm resolve. In such circumstances, it would be indeed astonishing if many political leaders had not been mere self-seekers; it would be rather more than astonishing since, until human nature is so changed as to be unrecognizable, very many political leaders in all lands will be of such a character.

Even so, however, the conception of the political life of the republics as being nothing more than a series of contests between mere adventurers is palpably untrue. It is to the last degree improbable that no men of any other type have ever attained to the direction of public affairs. It becomes not merely improbable, but impossible, when the material, the intellectual and the moral advance accomplished by these states in little more than a century is taken into consideration. Nor must it be forgotten that a leader is nothing unless he can secure adherents, and that no great measure of support will ever be accorded to those who fight only for their own hand. The devotion with which many of the leaders in the struggles of the republics have been followed is almost proof that those leaders were pursuing some higher object than their own advantage. That advantage they may have desired and probably did desire; they have been no more free from personal ambition than was a Richelieu or a Napoleon, a Cromwell or a Pitt. But in some cases, at the very least, they must have been also sincerely anxious to do their best for their country, even if their conception of that best has been mistaken, even if they have frequently confounded the best for their country with the best for themselves.

So unsatisfactory, indeed, is this interpretation of the political history of Spanish America that an alternative explanation has been put forward. It has been pointed out that the independence of the republics is of relatively recent date and that their inhabitants are thus inevitably lacking in political experience, their capacity for self-government naturally undeveloped. They have yet, it is urged, to learn the difference between liberty and licence; they have yet to understand that freedom, to be real, must be subjected to certain necessary restraints. Simon Bolivar himself laid down that for very many years an autocracy was the only feasible system of government for the states which had come into existence so very largely through his efforts. But his dictum was disregarded and a premature attempt was made to equip those states with institutions unsuited to the stage of development which their people had reached. That which might have been foreseen occurred. The republics have constantly tended to drift into a condition of anarchy; power in the hands of popular assemblies, untrained and inexperienced, has been misused; administration has been inefficient and corrupt, and political society has only been saved from dissolution by the application of drastic remedies, by reversion to a system better suited to the mentality of the citizens. While, however, they have been unable to attain the satisfactory working of more advanced institutions, the Spanish Americans have yet been able to appreciate the excellence of those institutions and to desire their con-tinued existence. Consequently, no sooner has some relief been gained from continuous misgovernment and disorder, than opposition has developed to the agency which brought such relief. To revolution has succeeded counter-revolution. 'Liberty' has been restored, only to degenerate once more into something akin to anarchy, from which the state has been again rescued by a return to autocracy. This unhappy process has been continued, until it has seemed that the normal condition of the republics is one of violent unrest and of perpetual changes of government.

In this conception of the political life of the Spanish American states there is a certain plausibility and a certain element of truth. The independence of the republics is of comparatively recent date and during the preceding period the direction of the central govern-ment assuredly did not rest with the population of the Spanish colonial empire. On the contrary, it was the considered policy of the Spanish crown to exclude from the highest offices of state in America even the creoles, men of pure European descent born in the New World. In the long list of over seven hundred and fifty viceroys, governors, and presidents of *audiencias*, less than twenty creoles appear. It is not less true that capacity for administration cannot be gained in a moment or from the mere study of treatises upon the art of government; for the smooth and satisfactory working of repre-sentative institutions some experience would appear to be essential. That many of the republics have at times drifted into a state of anarchy, that in many revolutions have been of very frequent occurrence, is mere matter of fact; that in all the republics autocratic interludes have occurred, and that in some at least these interludes have been the very salvation of society, is not

to be denied. Nor is it entirely unreasonable to suggest
that with greater political experience violent changes
in the system of government will cease, or that the
constitutions will then be far more generally maintained
in force.

At the same time this interpretation of the political
history of the republics will hardly bear critical ex-
amination. Broadly speaking, all the Spanish American
states are of the same age politically; their independence
dates from the same generation. It might therefore
be supposed that they would all have attained the same
degree of stability, if stability depended upon experience
in self-government or if instability were the result of
inexperience. It might also be supposed that if variations appeared, those states would be most liable to
revolutionary change which, in the colonial period,
were the least developed, the least fully settled. In
actual fact, however, neither the one supposition nor
the other is justified. In different republics, very different degrees of stability have been attained, nor is
it true that those lands which first attained independence are the most free from unrest. It is still less
true that the most settled states are those which in the
colonial period were most fully developed. The Argentine Republic and Uruguay to-day present examples of
stable government; Ecuador and Peru, of unrest. But
into a very large part of the territory now included in
the Argentine Republic, the Spaniards never pene-
trated at all; in many other districts they were obliged
to carry on an arduous warfare against Indian tribes
which were never fully subdued. Uruguay was even
less settled and controlled; the Spanish hold upon that
province was confined to Montevideo and to a few
other points and was constantly disputed by the Portuguese. On the other hand, Ecuador was very fully
subdued, while Peru was the seat of the principal viceroyalty and of the leading university, was the very

centre of Spanish culture, and was more completely settled and more completely developed than any other province.

It might, indeed, almost seem that the exact converse represents the truth; that stability has been most fully attained in those states which were least subjected to Spanish influence, and that to the baleful effect of Spanish misgovernment any present instability is to be attributed. But this suggested explanation is also in disaccord with facts. Throughout the colonial period, Chile was the scene of a long series of wars between the Spaniards and the Araucanians; the latter retained their independence to the last, and upon the southern half of the Spanish province the hold of Spain was at best precarious. The greater part of the modern republic of Bolivia was altogether unsubdued; the total Spanish population of the district was small and to-day the Spanish element in that population is far outnumbered by the Indian. Yet Chile has enjoyed relative stability, whereas Bolivia has not. It is in fact clear that neither political experience nor lack of such experience, neither development during the colonial period nor lack of such development, neither the presence nor the absence of a large Spanish element in the population, suffices to explain the political history of the republics or to account for that conflict of which they have been the scene.

This becomes still clearer when weight is given to considerations of a more general character. It is a fundamental truth that political changes cannot be brought about unless some principle, something higher than merely material interest, is invoked and is believed to be at issue. No revolution can occur unless at the very least it secures the support of a considerable minority of the population and such support cannot be gained if no appeal be made to sentiment or intellect. Some, and even very many, may be roused to action by

the promise or the hope of material gain; the mere
desire for better conditions of life, for more food, more
clothes, better housing, will be for some always a
sufficient motive. But the number of those for whom
it is sufficient will never constitute a majority in any
community; it will never constitute even a really
substantial minority.

There is no European people so indifferent to
political questions as the French, who are always ready
to commit the direction of public affairs to a small
minority and are careless of the form of government
under which they live, provided that they are allowed
peacefully to pursue their own avocations. Yet even
in France no revolution has been effected without
the adhesion to the revolutionary cause of a substantial
minority; the authors of every change have been
obliged to secure at least the support of the Paris mob.
To attain that support it has also been always necessary
to make an appeal, however insincere and however
hypocritical, to some ideal; it has been essential to
induce the belief that some abstract principle was at
stake. It was by means of such an appeal that the
revolutions of 1789, of 1830, of 1848 were effected.
It was not economic distress and financial chaos that
overthrew the Ancien Régime; the old order was destroyed by the declaration of the Rights of Man and in
pursuit of Liberté, Égalité, Fraternité. It was for the sake
of abstract liberty that Paris rose against Charles X;
it was in the same cause that Louis Philippe was
driven out. In each of these cases the spiritual and the
ideal were invoked; it was the absence of any such
invocation that rendered abortive the attempted revolution of Boulanger.

It may, perhaps, be argued that the French have
always tended to be swayed by mere words. Their
very genius for the crystallization of an idea in a happy
phrase has, perhaps, served to render them often in-

different to the actual implication of the idea itself;
the devotion which they appear to feel for a principle
is, perhaps, in reality excited by the phrase in which it
is embodied. But there is no nation upon earth less
moved by phrases and less attracted by mere abstractions
than the English, and yet in England, no less than in
France, every political change of moment has involved
some appeal to sentiment, the invocation of some principle. Political leaders, from the days of Simon de
Montfort onwards, have found it to be an essential of
success that their cause should be represented as being
something higher than any mere material gain. This
necessity was appreciated by Cromwell, by the authors
of the Revolution of 1688, by the advocates of the
Reform Bill of 1832; it was as fully appreciated by the
protagonists of the independence of the United States.
It was the lack of any such appeal to principle which
rendered the Chartist agitation so innocuous; it was
the materialism of its chief organizers which defeated
the General Strike of 1926.

And that which is true of two peoples, so radically
divergent in character as the French and the English,
is true of all other nations possessing a civilization of
European origin. Among such nations, when no
essential change results from the transference of power
from one party to another, when an alliance between
men of different parties is always possible, no vigorous
political life can really exist. It is only when there is a
divergence of principles, of ideals, that genuine contention occurs; such contention is not produced by the
strife of ambitions or by disagreement concerning mere
methods of government or by mere desire for some
material advantage, some purely economic change. The
stagnation of political life in France since the creation
of the Third Republic, the fact that between the various
groups of which the Chamber is composed there is
always the possiblity of coalition, the fact that between

these groups no real difference exists, is due to the
absence of any conflict of ideals. To the same cause may
be attributed the unreality of politics in the United
States, where, as in France, the professedly contending
parties are agreed upon all fundamental issues and are
almost driven to manufacture differences for the purpose of a presidential election.

In the same way, the continuously healthy political
life of England has been due to the fact that there
has always been such a division of principle between
two contending parties. Originally, such a division
existed between Conservatives and Liberals; to-day it
exists between Conservatives and Socialists, and the
decadence of the Liberal party may be attributed to
the belief, so widely held, that its leader found nothing
repugnant in the idea of an alliance with either the
extreme right or the extreme left, that his only motive
for action was a desire to secure power.

Whatever criticisms may be brought against the
conduct of political affairs in the Spanish American
republics it is undeniable that in them political life
is sufficiently vigorous. It may even be regarded as
somewhat too vigorous, since the conflict of parties has
been not infrequently transferred from the chamber to
the camp, and the issue decided not by counting heads
but by breaking them. So far from rival leaders being
normally ready enough to come to terms, it has
more often been true that exile and death have been
the penalty attaching to political defeat. The triumph
of a dictator has almost always been followed by the
proscription of the advocates of liberty; the overthrow
of a dictatorship has generally involved the banish-
ment or execution of the fallen despot. It is true that
such acts of violence might be expected as the outcome
of a conflict between two ambitious leaders; their mere
occurrence is not in itself evidence that any principle
has been at stake. The annals of the Roman Empire

afford abundant proof that the assassination of an auto-
crat may be merely the prelude to the exaltation of
another, that it may be the outcome of a mere palace
intrigue or of a mere military sedition. But it must be
remembered that, in the Spanish American countries,
conditions are very different from those which prevailed
in the Roman Empire or from those which prevail in the
military states of Europe. In no republic is the pro-
fessional army numerous; in all, revolutionary opera-
tions have been conducted very largely by volunteer
forces, compulsory enlistment in the rival bands being
only an occasional feature of these contests. The
adherents of the one party and of the other are men,
for the most part, who are ready to risk, if not to lay
down, their lives for the cause which they adopt. Even
in cases where the struggle has been waged by methods
so humanitarian that danger of death has been relatively
remote, there has always been the possibility of exile,
with resultant material loss and moral suffering, or of
confinement in prisons, which were not designed to
serve either as hotels or as sanatoria. Such willingness
to make sacrifices to a cause argues belief in that cause;
in the case of the rank and file it argues a very strong
belief, since for them the material advantages to be
secured from victory are smaller, both absolutely and
relatively, than those which may be gained by the
leaders. But for such a belief to be held by the majority
of any party it must also be believed that some principle
is involved. The divergence between the two parties
must thus be one of ideals; the conflict is in its nature
spiritual, not material, having its origin in a funda-
mentally different conception of the aim to be sought
in the organization of political society.

No sooner is it realized that such must be the nature
of the conflict between parties in the Spanish American
republics than the true character of that conflict
becomes apparent; it becomes obvious that it is a

contest between differing principles and differing ideals. Upon the one side are ranged those who are devoted to the principles of liberty which are expressed in the clauses of the constitutions and to establish which those constitutions were framed. They were convinced that, in the words of the Mexican constitution, 'Los derechos del hombre son la base y el objeto de las instituciones sociales.' For the sake of these rights it is worth while to lose all else; deprived of these rights no conceivable benefit can be of value. It is better to live in anarchy, in poverty, in misery, than to be in enjoyment of every material blessing, of law and good order, without freedom. Even the very dissolution of society is preferable to its organization upon an autocratic basis; for the sake of being free and equal every ill may be borne with cheerfulness. Such belief is the more readily entertained because it is associated with a lively hope of future good. While, without freedom, nothing really good can be possessed, full confidence is felt that if only freedom be cherished and preserved every good thing will ultimately be attained.

Upon the other side are ranged those who are not convinced that liberty in itself is the greatest good or that its attainment is the truest purpose of political association. Less attracted by abstract ideals, rather more alive to present evils and less confident of future blessings, they tend to consider rather the practical results of any system of government than its theoretical character. They are convinced that, before all things, security of life, limb, and property should be attained, that industry and commerce should be protected and fostered, and that material prosperity should be promoted, arguing that liberty, however desirable, is of little value if its possession involves the enduring of manifold ills. It is their conviction that the results which they desire can be most surely secured by the establishment of efficient government, and that it is therefore far more vital that government should be efficient than that it should be organized upon liberal or democratic principles. If compelled to make their choice between liberty, accompanied by disorder and verging upon licence, and political servitude, accompanied by good order, respect for law and that internal peace without which national prosperity is unattainable, they unhesitatingly choose the latter. They have accordingly been led to support despotic governments, regarding them as the means by which their conception of the truest good of the state can be best realized.

The population of the Spanish American republics is thus perpetually divided into two parties, each of which is actuated by devotion to a principle. The one holds that liberty, the other that efficient administration, is the greatest good. To the one, the diminution of the power of the executive is an end to be sought; to the other, the exaltation of that power. To the one, the rights of the individual are all important; to the other, the stability of the state. It is not that the one deliberately seeks the disintegration of society, or that the other deliberately seeks the oppression of the private citizen, but that the one would prefer disintegration to tyranny, and the other tyranny to disintegration.

Herein consists that conflict which has constituted the political life of these states. It is no mere contest of ambitions to be ended when men have learned to restrain within reasonable bounds their pursuit of their own interest. It is not merely the outcome of lack of experience in self-government, to be ended when such experience has been gained. It is emphatically a conflict of principles, both parties in which are equally sincere and equally inspired by devotion to an ideal. It is therefore also a conflict which can cease only when means have been discovered whereby liberty and efficiency, the stability of the state and the rights of individuals, can be simultaneously secured.

II

LIBERTY AND EFFICIENCY

THE existence in all the Spanish American states, save Panama on the mainland and the island republics, of such contention between those who set liberty, and those who set efficient government, before all else in the political sphere is not the outcome of any transitory circumstances. It is the product of the temperament of the peoples of these states, and its origin is therefore to be sought in a period anterior to the discovery of the continent by Columbus, not in the New World, but in the Old, not in the republics themselves, but in their motherland, Spain.

It is perhaps hardly realized in Europe to-day that the Spanish empire in America was at once the greatest, the most enduring, and, in many respects, the most remarkable colonial empire which the world has yet seen. It extended from northward of San Francisco to southward of Buenos Aires; it comprised within its limits Mexico and all Central America, and a very large part both of South America and of the southern and western districts of the present United States. It endured, with no serious diminution of area, for some three hundred years, a fact which is the more notable when it is remembered that during by far the greater part of that period Spain was in a condition of decline, that she was defeated in war after war, and that her American possessions were assailed by the French, the English, and the Dutch.

Nor is it altogether easy to appreciate the extent to which, while her empire yet endured, Spain impressed upon it her own essential characteristics, or to realize that there is to-day between her and her daughter states in the New World a spiritual bond, which is rather the stronger than the weaker because the former political bond has been so completely severed. To her dominions across the Atlantic Spain gave all that was hers to give, and her gifts have been cherished by those who received them. In every land from the Rio Grande to Tierra del Fuego, with the important exception of Brazil and the minor exceptions of British Honduras and the Guianas, the basis of all culture is to-day Spanish. In all those lands Spanish is the official, the literary, and the commercial language; save in Paraguay, in a large part of Bolivia and in some remoter districts of other states, it is also the language of everyday intercourse for the vast mass of the population. The manners and customs of the people of the republics are ultimately Spanish in origin. If in the greater cities and among the wealthier sections of the community, dress is fashioned upon the models of London or Paris, yet it is from Spain that the overwhelming majority even of the women of these states derive the inspiration of their personal adornment. The dominant religious creed is equally Spanish; the special characteristics of Spanish Catholicism are faithfully reproduced. Even that agnosticism which appears is rather the agnosticism of Spain than that of England or France or the United States, having a political colouring which is not found in those lands. The whole intellectual outlook of the Spanish Americans is, indeed, ultimately traceable to Spain. It is true that this outlook has been sensibly modified by differing conditions of life, and that it has been subjected to non-Spanish influences. But its fundamental characteristics are yet derived from that land which gave to America its first schools and its oldest university.

To the New World also the Spaniards carried their political ideas, and in every land which they conquered and settled was reproduced that special political problem by which Spain herself has been perplexed all through the ages. By that problem the peoples of the republics have been equally absorbed; their political, no less than their intellectual, outlook has been determined by their Spanish origin. Here again, it may be admitted, that something has been drawn from other sources. The repercussions of the French Revolution were felt in Spanish America; the provisions of the constitutions of the republics are in very many instances couched in phraseology familiar enough to any one who has read the orations delivered in the Constituent Assembly and in the Convention, or who has read some of the pamphlet literature which poured in so unending a stream from the printing-presses of revolutionary Paris. The form of the institutions which have been established in these states is to a very great extent English, borrowed from England directly or indirectly through the United States. But it is neither in Paris nor in London nor in Washington that the true origin of the political outlook of Spanish America is to be found. The verbal expression of ideas may be French; the forms by which it is sought to translate those ideas into action may be English, but the ideas themselves, their underlying spirit, all that converts words into something more than mere verbiage, and that gives vitality to otherwise dead forms, is Spanish.

It is because that underlying spirit is Spanish, because in the political, no less than in every other, aspect of life in these states Spanish influences are still predominant, that there exists in them a perpetual conflict between love of liberty and love of efficiency. That self-same conflict existed in Spain long before Columbus sailed the Atlantic; it determined the political history of Castile in an age when men as yet hardly dreamed that the ocean was navigable, and when they dismissed as idle fancies vague conjectures concerning the existence of habitable and inhabited lands to the westward. Even in a period so remote that the very names of Aragon and Castile were yet to be heard for the first time, the peoples of the Iberian peninsula were already perplexed by this problem, were already the prey of these conflicting emotions. The conflict was, indeed, born in them; it forms a vital part of their very nature, and when they crossed the Atlantic they could do no other than bear it with them to the lands which they came to inhabit.

From the very earliest times a love of individual liberty and local freedom has been instinctive to the Spanish race. Nothing could be more erroneous than to suppose that the Spaniards are or have ever been a people generally submissive to external control, careless of the right to order their own lives. On the contrary, there is perhaps no nation in Europe to whom liberty has been so dear, who have been so impatient of authority, or so resolute in resistance to even the most salutary restraints upon freedom. The very physical characteristics of a great part of the peninsula, and more especially the physical characteristics of Castile, seemed to foster a spirit of local independence and to breed a race of men so fiercely devoted to their personal liberty as to be almost habitually turbulent in its defence. Rugged mountain ranges and swiftly flowing rivers, peculiarly liable to sudden flood, cut up the country, between the different parts of which communication was never easy and was often practically impossible. The various districts, isolated from one another, were averse from any form of union, mutually suspicious or mutually hostile, nor was there any clearly determined centre round which, by sentiment or by economic necessity, they were moved or compelled to rally. From a somewhat ungenerous soil, scorched by the sun in summer and devastated by icy storms in winter, only a hard livelihood could be wrested. The bitterness and the persistence of this struggle with nature inspired the race with self-reliance, rendering it warlike and courageous, strenuous and enduring, rendering it also impatient of control, prone to violence

and disorder, proudly free in spirit. For the Castilian
there was no certain hope of any adequate reward for
labour; the product of months of arduous toil might
well vanish in one night of tempest. But if the land
offered to its inhabitants neither rich fields to culti-
vate nor smiling plains to till, it offered to them
in exchange an abundance of strongholds needing no
art to fortify them, safe lairs in which they might be
secure from their enemies and from which they might
readily issue forth to prey upon their fellows. Nature
herself seemed to urge them to care each for himself
alone, to refuse submission to others, almost to disbelieve
in either the necessity or the advantage of any form
of political association, to care nothing for peace or
good order.

The lesson, so taught by nature, was reinforced by
experience. It was to local and individual, rather than
to national and concerted, effort that Spain had owed
the most glorious achievements of her past. Numantia
had for years resisted single-handed all the power of
Rome; the cities of the Roman province, acting in-
dependently of one another, had stayed for a while the
advance of the barbarian invaders of the peninsula.
After the Saracen conquest, it was by the isolated
Christian groups in the mountains of the north that the
fire of independence was kept burning. It was by the
efforts of individual leaders, far more truly than by
those of national forces, that the Moors were gradually
driven back until they were confined within the narrow
limits of the kingdom of Granada. El Cid Campeador
himself, the darling hero of medieval Spain, was the
captain of a private army, fighting for his own hand
and being upon occasion in opposition to the monarchy
which he might be supposed to obey and even to the
Faith of which he was the professed champion. Inch
by inch, territory was regained by those who relied upon
themselves, who kept that which they had won by their

own might, and whose memory is enshrined in the very
name of the country which they reconquered and held,
Castilla, the land of castles.

By their very dependence upon their own efforts,
whether in the arts of peace or in those of war, that
free spirit, innate in the race and in accord with the
nature of the country, was continuously fostered. An
intense localism became markedly characteristic of
Spain, and more especially of so much of Spain as was
comprised within the kingdom of Castile. There was
always a marked reluctance to combine even against
the common enemy, save when for a moment a wave
of religious enthusiasm swept over the country; the
forces of the Christians were constantly divided and
their arms directed not against the Moors but against
one another. Aragon, León, Castile and Navarre were
more frequently hostile, than friendly, states; union
between them, when momentarily effected, was speedily
dissolved, and until the marriage of Ferdinand and
Isabella, only Castile and Leon were permanently
united. The protagonists in the struggles between the
rival kingdoms were often ready to call the infidel to
their aid; the bond of a common Christianity was dissolved that local animosities might be gratified.

Nor was there unity within the individual states.
Down to the reign of Ferdinand and Isabella, Castile
was more especially the scene of civil strife and was
in a condition of almost perpetual anarchy. The monarchy was again and again attacked by the nobles;
between the various nobles, private wars were of frequent occurrence. The greater landowners, lay and
ecclesiastical alike, were practically independent sovereigns on their own estates, maintaining private armies
and exercising all regalian rights. The cities and towns
enjoyed a very wide measure of autonomy; petty lords
of castles gathered round them bands of followers and
roamed over the countryside, robbing and pillaging and

murdering, rendering unsafe all ways of communication. Royal authority was reduced to a shadow; if a strong king could for a moment enforce obedience, such obedience was yielded only under compulsion and the habit of submission was not thereby induced. Law itself was local, not national; the *fueros*, collections of the customs and privileges of communities, were as varied as they were numerous and were in their essence so many charters of individual liberty, so many expressions of the inveterate localism of the race.

Love of personal and local freedom was by no means destroyed when its open expression was rendered impossible by the development and consolidation of royal power under Ferdinand and Isabella and under the first two monarchs of the Austrian house. After the defeat of the *comuneros*, no further open resistance to the crown was offered in Castile; as at an earlier date the nobles had been subdued, so now municipal independence was extinguished. The Cortes ceased to play any part in administration or legislation; its protests were half-hearted and ineffective, and it became little, if anything, more than a machine for registering the royal will. But the spirit of liberty survived the establishment of autocracy; it was perhaps stifled, but it was not slain. It inspired the resistance offered, during the War of the Spanish Succession, to the attempt to impose a sovereign upon the country by force of foreign arms. It was responsible for the sustained and ultimately triumphant opposition to Napoleon, for the heroism of a struggle in which Zaragoza recalled the glory of Numantia. The same spirit survives in the country to-day. One of the most serious difficulties of every Spanish government in recent times has been that which was a difficulty to the governments of the Middle Ages. It has been the unending task of every ruler to discover some solution for the problem presented by the intense localism of the people, by their reluctance to subordinate their personal and individual freedom even to the highest considerations of the general good.

This localism and this passion for individual liberty would, indeed, have effectually prevented the organization of Spain into a single state had it not been counteracted by another sentiment, almost, if not quite, as strong and equally innate and permanent. The Spanish race has always inclined to worship efficiency in every walk of life, to applaud whole-heartedly any actor upon the stage of affairs who performs his part effectively, no matter what that part may be and no matter what may be the result of its effective performance. To those who are possessed of outstanding ability, ungrudging admiration has always been willingly accorded and something more than mere admiration, even when the ability has been exercised in opposition to the cherished ideas of the race. Such admiration and devotion has been accorded in the political as in all other spheres. If Spain offered the most strenuous resistance to the establishment of Roman rule, it also became the most fully Romanized of all the provinces of the empire; it fought for its liberty; it admired that effective organization by which its liberty was destroyed. Of the long line of Spanish sovereigns those whose memory is most cherished are those who were most autocratic; Ferdinand and Isabella, who crushed aristocratic and undermined municipal independence; Charles V and Philip II, who consolidated despotism; Charles III, benevolent despot, of whom it has been said, 'no puede pronunciarse sin un sentimiento de amor respetuoso el nombre'; even Ferdinand VII, disreputable tyrant though he was, 'el mucho rey'. In Spain, political capacity fulfils that function which is usually assigned to charity; it does indeed cover a multitude of sins. The very race which is most passionately devoted to liberty is also the very race which is most ready to admire and to submit to despotism. Between these two sentiments, there is an

inevitable conflict, and that conflict is the more sustained because each sentiment is so intensely felt,
because almost every Spaniard, and perhaps every true
Spaniard, feels both equally acutely, because the conflict proceeds not only in the land in which he lives but
in his own heart and mind also.

That emotions so apparently contradictory should
be felt by one and the same individual at one and the
same time, that a passionate love of liberty should be
combined with a passionate admiration for despotism,
is more readily explicable than might be supposed. At
first sight the Spaniard appears to be prone to extra-
vagance of all kinds. The phraseology, in which expression is given to devotion to the fair, seems to the
mind of less emotional races to border upon the
ridiculous. The very language of ordinary social intercourse is exaggerated in comparison with that of the
colder climates of the north. It very obviously cannot
represent with accuracy either the sentiments or the
intentions of those by whom it is used; when a guest
is informed that the house of his host and all that it
contains is his, no transference of ownership is contemplated. So palpable, indeed, does the exaggeration
appear to be that it has been sometimes regarded as
indicative of an insincerity equal to that which is the
hall-mark of the Celtic races. But any such supposition
is unjustified. Used by a Spaniard, such language, while
not to be given its literal meaning, is every whit as
sincere in intention as are the more restrained phrases of
the Teutonic peoples. It is the expression of a national
characteristic, of that idealism which inspires all the
thought and all the action of the Spanish people.

For, of all peoples upon earth, the Spanish is perhaps
the most idealistic. Everything is idealized; there is a
fervent desire that all should be ideal. Love should be
ideal love, complete, absolute, unbounded; the lover
should be in all things the slave of his mistress, sur-

rendering to her his whole being, body, soul and spirit. Friendship should be ideal; social intercourse should become that of friends, not of mere acquaintances. For the mediocre and the commonplace there is no place in the mind of the Spaniard; in all things he strives towards perfection, and with anything less than perfection he remains wholly dissatisfied.

To attain perfection, Spain has in the past been ready to spend her last maravedi and to shed the last drop of her blood; for the ideal, the race has been ready to lay down its very life. For centuries the Spanish people waged an arduous contest with the Moorish possessors of the soil of the peninsula, fighting far less for mere territory or mere booty than in order to achieve the complete triumph of that creed which they had so ardently embraced and in which they found the ideal expression of the relationship between man and his Maker. It was to attain the ideal of complete orthodoxy that the fires of the Inquisition were lighted and that the Jews and the Moriscoes were expelled. It was for the sake of an ideal that Spain endeavoured to impose her moral hegemony upon Europe, that the forces of Christendom might be perfectly united against the enemies of the Saviour of the world. In prosecution of this mission she sent forth the best of her manhood to conquer, to settle, and to convert the inhabitants of the New World. In prosecution of this same mission Alba established the Tribunal of Blood, and for eighty years Spain vainly strove to subdue the resistance of the Dutch. In the same cause war after war was waged against France, the Armada dispatched against England. So powerful was the devotion of the pursuit of the ideal, that in the darkest period of Spanish history her soldiers went forth willingly to die that it might triumph, though they were ill-led, ill-clothed, ill-fed, and unpaid. So powerful was that devotion that Spain, experiencing to the full all the ill effects of a most pernicious

financial system, with her industries ruined and her
fields untilled, yet struggled to attain, entering into
conflicts in which she had no concern save that the
cause which she embraced was to her the cause of an
ideal orthodoxy.

It is in this idealism that the explanation of the
apparent contradiction is to be found. The Spaniard
loves liberty, that ideal liberty for which there is no
place in an imperfect world. He would be free to the
very fullest extent, free in a wider sense than is in
fact compatible with the continued existence of organized society. He would be master of all his own actions;
he would order as he wills every relation of his life;
he would be delivered from even the mildest and most
necessary restraint. He is, indeed, a passionate individualist, aspiring to attain an ideal individualism
which is attainable only, in the phrase of Aristotle,
either by a brute or a god.

But side by side with this passion for liberty is found
recognition of the fact that government is a necessity
and a consequent desire that government also should
be ideal. The function of the ruler is to rule. He must
therefore rule fully, absolutely, exerting his authority
without restraint and upon all in every relationship of
life. He must be a despot or nothing, for if he be less
than a despot, he is forthwith imperfect, mediocre.
He fails, if he be not absolute, to perform in the most
complete manner those functions to perform which
he exists; he falls short of the ideal. That very individualism which impels the Spaniard to resist control
leads him also to welcome control when it is the result
of a vigorous assertion of individuality by another;
the more vigorous the assertion, the more ready his
submission. And hence, there is a perpetual tendency
to alternate between a degree of liberty which amounts
almost to the negation of all government and a degree
of government which amounts almost to a negation

of all liberty. This alternation, and the conflict of which it is the result, is the inevitable product of the Spanish mind, of the combination of love of freedom with love of efficient government, of that ardent ideal- ism by which the race has always been inspired. And it is to the nature of the temperament of the race that the apparent contradictions of the political life of Spanish America, the conflict which constitutes that life, must be ultimately traced.

III

THE CHARACTER OF THE SPANISH EMPIRE

THE Spanish Empire in America endured for almost three hundred years; the work of conquest, save in the modern Argentine Republic, was practically completed before the end of the first half of the sixteenth century and it was in the first quarter of the nineteenth century that the independence of the republics was achieved. During the whole of that period the empire suffered no serious loss of territory. A certain number of West Indian islands passed into other hands, and some sentimental grief at least was experienced when Haiti, the cradle of Spanish dominion in the New World, became a French possession. Part of Honduras was occupied by the English; English, French, and Dutch were established in the Guianas, but neither in the one district nor in the other had Spanish rule ever been enforced, while in the case of Guiana dominion was hardly claimed. Nothing, indeed, which was really valued, was lost. The hold of Spain upon Mexico and Peru, upon the mainland generally, was never seriously threatened and was in no sense destroyed. It is a somewhat noteworthy fact that, upon the very eve of its final dissolution, Spanish dominion in America attained its greatest territorial extension, Louisiana being received from France at the end of the Seven Years War and Florida being recovered from England at the close of the War of American Independence.

Spain preserved her empire, moreover, in circumstances in which such preservation might have been judged to be impossible. In the whole course of history there can hardly be a more curious phenomenon than that which is here presented. A state, itself sinking below the level of a second-rate power, maintained

intact its imperial position and maintained that position
not by vigorous effort, not by force of arms, not by
chance immunity from attack, not by the aid of powerful allies, but solely because the provinces of which its
empire was composed had no desire to sever the ties
binding them to the mother country and had assuredly
still less desire to substitute the rule of any other
nation for that of the nation by which they had been
originally acquired and settled.

The absence of any such desire appears at first sight
to be sufficiently remarkable. There seem to be abundant reasons why the colonies should have yearned to
be free from the dominion of Spain. Misgovernment
was rife enough. Despite the energy and devotion of
many of the viceroys and governors, it cannot be
seriously contended that Spain sent to the New World
a number of exceptionally capable administrators. The
majority of those entrusted with the government of her
American possessions were rather magnificent than
efficient; they entirely failed to leave behind them a
grateful memory of solid achievement or a record of
admirable work ably accomplished. As, among the
conquistadores, few, except Cortés, compare favourably
with a Clive or a Warren Hastings, so, among the many
viceroys, it is perhaps only Francisco de Toledo who
merits comparison with a Lord Lawrence. Administration was generally feeble and not infrequently corrupt
at the centre; in local affairs the tyranny and oppression
of minor officials was notorious.

The inhabitants of the provinces, indeed, laboured
under an accumulation of grievances in comparison
with which those which produced the revolt of the
English colonies in North America may be regarded as
having been to a degree trivial. The creoles were
almost entirely excluded from high official positions:
in the administration of their own affairs they had at
best no more than a subordinate share. That their

exclusion from office was resented long before the
movement for independence began is illustrated by the
somewhat pathetic memorial addressed by one of their
number to Philip V. They were not less relegated to
an inferior social position, their disabilities of this kind
being, perhaps, a greater source of discontent than those
of a political nature. The lot of the *mestizos*, those of
mixed Spanish and Indian blood, was even less to be
envied. They were socially and almost legally suspended
between the Heaven, reserved for 'Europeans', those
who had been born in Spain, and the Hell, to which
the natives were often consigned; for them, descent to
the Hell was far easier and infinitely more probable
than ascent to the Heaven. Of the other elements in
the population, the *zambos*, those with an admixture
of negro blood, were in a worse position than the
mestizos; the pure negroes were actual slaves. The
Indians, save such of their number as succeeded in
preserving a savage freedom, were in general subjected
to compulsory labour and were in a condition of legally
recognized inferiority. The sorrows of this last class
have certainly been exaggerated and were largely the
result of their inordinate fondness for ardent spirits of
atrocious quality. The care for their moral welfare
displayed by the kings and by the religious orders and
for their material welfare as illustrated by the number
of regulations safeguarding their interests and by the
provision of institutions, schools, and hospitals, for
their benefit, must be recognized. But both in the
mines and in the manufactories, in the latter of which
they were often placed under inhuman negro super-
visors, their condition was constantly deplorable, and
at its very best was not such as to inspire them with any
deep affection for Spanish rule.

Over the inhabitants generally, and more especially
over the Spanish and *mestizo* sections of the population,
the Church exercised an authority which was sometimes

resisted and which was more often resented. To the introduction of the Inquisition somewhat general opposition was offered and was successful in the province of Buenos Aires; everywhere the Indians were exempted from its jurisdiction in deference to the plea that it would be unreasonable to expect from them that rigid orthodoxy which might be legitimately demanded from those in a higher state of intellectual development. The government frowned upon all free expression of opinion, unless, perhaps, that opinion was expressed in memorials addressed to the crown or to the Council of the Indies. It looked coldly upon any indulgence of a taste for secular learning; one viceroy of Peru was removed from his position mainly because he extended his patronage to a literary society at Lima. The censorship of all printed matter was vested in ecclesiastical hands and was rigorously exercised. The production of books in Spanish America was severely restricted; the importation of books was almost prohibited, since in the opinion of those responsible there were relatively few authors whose writings were not wholly pernicious or at least unsuitable for colonial readers. All speculative works were more especially proscribed; the writings of the political thinkers of the eighteenth century were in general introduced into Spanish America only by the employment of the artifice of binding them in the covers of books of religious devotion. From the Dutch island of Curaçao and from the English possessions in the West Indies a certain amount of prohibited literature was undoubtedly smuggled into the colonies, and there is reason to believe that this illicit trade was often carried on with the connivance of the civil authorities, jealous of the power of the Church. In the reign of the enlightened despots, Ferdinand VI and Charles III, there was some relaxation of the censorship, but it was Charles IV who declared that reading was an accomplishment with which the inhabitants of Spanish America could better dispense.

Education was more completely in the hands of the Church. It would be grossly unjust not to admit the excellence of the instruction given by the Jesuits and their devotion to the work which was entrusted mainly to them. But at the same time it would be a fallacy to suppose that they permitted those ideas which were so eagerly debated in eighteenth-century Europe to be freely canvassed in the universities and schools under their control. The education which they provided became, indeed, increasingly unsatisfying to the more restless minds eager to be informed on the latest speculations of European free-thinkers. Many of the more fortunately circumstanced creoles proceeded to France in order to acquire that knowledge which they could not obtain at home. Such emigration was discountenanced by the authorities and those who returned from the Old World were regarded with some suspicion. Their number nevertheless increased and the consequent permeation of new ideas into the Spanish colonies served to intensify resentment that the free propagation of those ideas was not permitted and to arouse a sense of grievance against the whole educational system.

Restraint of intellectual activity was not a grievance felt except by that relatively small class that could appreciate its existence. The grievances arising from the economic policy of Spain were felt by all free sections of the community to a greater or lesser degree. Even the Indians were here concerned, if only because they were compelled to expend no small part of their meagre wages on the purchase of linen drawers, which they did not wish to wear, and of razors useless to a beardless, and needles useless to a naked, population. During a great part of the colonial period the importation of commodities was legally confined to those of Spanish origin and could proceed only through certain ports in Spain and America. The supply of goods was constantly inadequate to meet the demand for them; the difficulty of transportation was extreme, and in much of Spanish South America the merchants of Lima enjoyed a monopoly of distribution which they jealously guarded. Prices rose to an irrationally high level and the price demanded was the more unreasonable because the bulk of almost every consignment from Europe was so damaged in transit as to be of little value when it ultimately reached its destination in the colonies.

A further grievance was produced by the restrictions imposed upon economic intercourse between the various Spanish possessions and upon the development of colonial industry. The growth of such intercourse and industry was feared by the home government both upon political and economic grounds. It was suspected that any advance in the direction of economic independence might foster a desire for political independence also; it was equally suspected that the formation of any close commercial ties between the various provinces might lead them to offer a combined resistance to the continued domination of Madrid. It was believed that any rise of manufactures in Spanish America would be prejudicial to the industries of Spain and would further lead to the withdrawal of necessary labour from the mines, the exploitation of which was always regarded as being of paramount importance to the home country. Hence, although trade between Mexico and the Philippines was permitted, and although mercury was exported from Peru for the refining of gold and silver in other provinces, and although the traffic in mules across the Andes from the province of Tucumán was considerable, intercolonial trade generally was prohibited or at least greatly discouraged; one viceroy of Peru was removed from office because he had allowed a vessel from the Philippines to discharge a cargo at one of the ports of his viceroyalty. Some encouragement was given to agriculture and to the production of such crops as were necessary for the support of the population or as could not be raised in Spain, but there was no serious effort to make full use of the fertility of the soil and of climatic advantages. The growing of any product which might be exported from Spain was forbidden; oliveyards were destroyed by the government in order that colonial might not enter into competition with Spanish oil. Despite the fact that the manufacturers of the home country became less and less able to supply the needs of a growing population in America, local production of necessary manufactured articles was as far as possible prevented.

It must be admitted that some relief from these varied economic grievances was actually secured during the colonial period, partly by the action of the creoles themselves, partly by that of foreigners, partly by that of the home government. Despite discouragement and even prohibition, a number of industries came into being; the textile manufactures of Peru attained some prosperity, and many commodities for local consumption were locally produced. The attempted restriction of importation was as unsuccessful as might have been expected when the extent and needs of the colonists, and the relative impotence of the Spanish government, are considered. Smuggling became general and was rather permitted than suppressed by the colonial authorities, many of whom derived considerable gain from their laxity in the enforcement of the law and some of whom were doubtless inspired by sympathy with the grievances of those whom they governed. From Colonia in Uruguay, whenever the Portuguese were in possession of that much-disputed place, commodities were distributed to the neighbouring Spanish provinces. The Dutch, having occupied Curaçao, carried on a very lucrative contraband trade with the mainland of northern South America; Puerto Cabello was created to serve as a point for the reception of smuggled goods. After their conquest of Jamaica the English entered the same field; their originally illicit trade with the Spanish colonies on the mainland received some shadow of authorization after the War of the Spanish Succession. By a clause in the Treaty of Utrecht, England was allowed to send one ship to the annual fair of Porto Bello, to which place Spanish vessels conveying goods for South America were obliged to proceed and where merchants congregated to receive the consignments. No provision was made against the replenishment of the cargo of the English vessel; she was therefore stationed for the whole period of the fair in the harbour and was constantly restocked by means of other vessels plying to and from Jamaica. In the same period, by the Asiento Treaty, the monopoly of the supply of negro slaves for Spanish America was conceded to the English who were permitted to sell to the colonists any surplus cargo from the slave-carrying ships. That surplus was amazingly large when the conditions in which the negroes were transported are considered, and under colour of this agreement, the English secured a foremost share in the markets of a large part of Spanish America. The legal restraints upon the importation of commodities had, indeed, become practically obsolete before the end of the colonial period.

In some measure those restraints had been modified by the action of government itself. The accession of a French prince, Philip V, to the Spanish throne was followed by the opening of colonial trade to France. After the signature of the Treaty of Utrecht an attempt was made by the establishment of a coastguard service to check the contraband trade carried on by the English; the disputes which followed culminated in the 'Jenkins' Ear War', and upon the conclusion of peace, Charles III endeavoured to regain trade for Spain by the adoption of a more liberal policy. Despite the modifications which he introduced, however, the colonies still had grounds for complaint at least as substantial as had the English colonies in North America against the operation of the Navigation Laws.

For the existence of such social, intellectual and economic grievances, no compensation was supplied, according to any ordinary standards, by the character of the Spanish administration of the colonies, of which inefficiency and disorder appeared to be the most outstanding features. The basis of the system established was the creation of checks and balances, by means of which it was believed that the hold of Spain upon her distant possessions might be most effectually secured. From the days of Columbus, who was accused of intending to transfer Haiti to the Genoese, of Cortés and Pizarro, who were regarded with suspicion on the ground of their very eminence, the home government displayed a constant nervousness lest the New World might slip from its grasp. It was feared that if any governor were invested with anything approaching a wide measure of undisputed authority, his loyalty would not be proof against the temptations of ambition, that the hatred for control, inherent in the race, would find expression in revolt, if there were any likelihood that revolt would be successful. That there should be no such likelihood, an effort was made to retain the ultimate direction even of the most seemingly trivial matters in the hands of the crown, an effort wholly in accord with those despotic principles which inspired the sovereigns of the House of Austria.

In Spain itself there was a persistent conflict of jurisdiction between the Council of the Indies and the Casa de Contratación. To the former, originally a species of committee of the Royal Council of Castile, and later developed into a distinct body, was nominally confided the general task of supervising the administration of the Spanish possessions and of drawing up such regulations as were needed for their government. To the latter was entrusted the duty of directing all economic intercourse between Spain and the New World. In their very nature, the spheres of activity of the two bodies were thus not entirely distinct; the exact frontier between political and economic questions was incapable of definition. Inasmuch as the Indies were chiefly valued as a source whence revenue might be derived, the tendency was always for the Casa to grow in importance and to secure a far greater share in the management of colonial affairs than that possessed by the Council. The differentiation of the two bodies was, however, maintained; it was never certain that the decisions of the one would not be disputed or reversed by the other. For ultimate decision, therefore, everything had to be referred to the crown and, while in the reign of so laborious a king as Philip II such reference was assured of attention, in the reigns of his successors, delays were multiplied and the attainment of any decision increasingly difficult.

The confusion of the spheres of authority of the Council and the Casa was, to some extent, accidental, and the conflict of authority between them was perhaps hardly anticipated when they were successively created. Indeed, in the earliest years of the colonial period, both bodies, in their embryonic form, were directed by a single individual, Juan Rodriguez de Fonseca, whose name is remembered as that of one who was consistently hostile to Columbus. On the other hand, the conflict of jurisdiction in the New World was not accidental but designed. It was the deliberate policy of those responsible for the organization of the government of Spanish America to deny to any official, however highly placed, freedom of action even within his own province, to make every official in some degree subordinate to some other official or body, in order that all might be kept in dependence upon the home government.

During the greater part of the colonial period two viceroys, those of Peru and Mexico, were at the head of administration in America; each was independent of the other, the slightly superior status of the viceroy of Peru, indicated by his larger salary, carrying with it no greater authority and no right of control over his fellow-viceroy. As representing the person of the sovereign and as being responsible for the promulgation of royal edicts, as the immediate superior of the provincial governors, as commander-in-chief of all the armed forces of the colonies, and as president in his own immediate province of the *audiencia*, the supreme judicial body, the viceroy occupied a position of incontestable dignity and great apparent power. But both by accidental circumstances and by deliberate regulation his authority was greatly circumscribed.

The mere extent of the territory over which he presided rendered it impossible that he should in actual fact exercise any permanent control over matters of detail. No viceroy of Peru ever made himself personally acquainted with all the districts within his viceroyalty; Francisco de Toledo, who did perhaps wish to do so and who travelled very extensively, was unable to do more than visit some part of the provinces of Peru, Quito and Charcas; the majority both of his predecessors and successors knew little more than Lima and its vicinity. The viceroys of Mexico journeyed through the country from Vera Cruz to their capital; they occasionally acquired a passing acquaintance with some of the West Indian islands and with some of the ports of Central America. But for their knowledge of the greater part of the lands which they were supposed to govern they were content to rely upon the reports which they received. It was, in such circumstances, inevitable that a very wide measure of local autonomy in relation to the viceroy had to be accorded to the provincial governors. Intervention from Lima or

Mexico in provincial affairs was fitful and was in general occasioned by the occurrence of some notable event which emphatically demanded action on the part of the viceroy.

Even, however, if distance had not presented so insuperable an obstacle to direct control the viceroy would have been unable effectively to direct the affairs of the various provinces. For while in name the governors were his subordinates, while at times he might actually exercise control over them, the subordination was imperfect and the control might be and was legally questioned. The Council of the Indies communicated directly with the governors, constantly sending to them instructions which were not transmitted through Lima or Mexico. Appeal to the authorities in Spain against a viceregal mandate was not only permitted but encouraged, and since the viceroy was uncertain of his ability to enforce compliance with orders which he might issue, he somewhat naturally inclined to refrain from issuing them. Indeed, long before the original viceroyalties were formally partitioned, the remoter of the provinces of which they were composed were virtually independent of viceregal control; even in the districts nearest to Lima or Mexico that control was rarely exerted.

Nor was the power of the viceroy by any means complete within the narrower limits of the province in which he resided, and of which he was the immediate governor. Appointed only for a short term, he was rarely able to make his personality felt, the less so because in almost every case he was a complete stranger to the land which he was required to administer, and was more often selected primarily for his social position rather than for his proved capacity. He was, moreover, obliged at the end of his period of office to submit to a *residencia*, that judicial inquiry into conduct to which all Spanish officials were subjected, and however salu-

tary this institution may have been in its intention and
however effective at times in preventing or punishing
abuses of power, there is no doubt that it contributed
to induce an excessive caution in the exercise of
authority. A retiring viceroy was little disposed to
risk a prolonged postponement of his return to Spain,
such as might be imposed upon him if by vigorous performance of his duties and by independence of attitude, he had given offence to any large number of individuals. He was rather inclined to act in such a manner
as to conciliate all interests, or at least all interests the
hostility of which might prove to be inconvenient at
the time of the *residencia*.

Frequent changes in the holders of the viceregal
office further weakened the viceregal position. It is
true that the memorial which each viceroy prepared
for his successor served in general to guide that successor's conduct and hence tended to produce a certain
continuity of policy. But the effect so produced was
very largely neutralized by the constantly occurring
interregna, during which the powers of the viceroy were
exercised by the *audiencia* of Lima or of Mexico, as
the case might be. The *audiencia* seemed almost to
delight in reversing as far as possible every act of the
last viceroy, and hence in depriving the policy of the
government of such coherence as it might otherwise
have possessed.

The independent or hostile attitude of the judicial
body imposed a serious check upon the authority of
the viceroy, even during his term of office. This was
the more so because the *audiencia* was empowered to
communicate directly with the Council of the Indies
and the Casa de Contratación, and constantly used this
power to the prejudice of the viceroy. He presided
over the deliberations of the judicial body, but was
not a member of it and had no voice in its decisions.
Orders which he issued might be and often were

nullified by the refusal of the *audiencia* to convict those who infringed their provisions; the viceroy had no power to compel the judicial authorities to administer the law or to render him that degree of support without which effective government was hardly within the range of possibility.

He was, however, as well able to thwart the *audiencia* as the *audiencia* was able to thwart him. If that body issued a judicial decision, the enforcement of the decision lay in the hands of the viceroy who might deliver from prison those who had been consigned to it. Since an almost perpetual state of enmity existed between the judges and the executive, laws were far more generally honoured in the breach than in the observance. Nor was this less the case when, during the vacancy of the viceregal office, the *audiencia* temporarily occupied the place of the viceroy. For the execution of its commands it was still driven to depend upon the *cabildo*, the council of each municipality, which controlled the police force, and the *cabildos* were as jealous of domination by the *audiencia* as the *audiencia* was jealous of domination by the viceroy. There was, in short, a general absence of coercive power. In the last resort, everything needed to be referred to Spain, and amid the interminable delays imposed by appeals and counter-appeals, stagnation was normally produced.

The attainment of efficient government was rendered even more difficult owing to the position occupied by the ecclesiastical authorities. Directly dependent upon the crown, and strong in their possession of the weapon of spiritual discipline, the bishops in every province were disposed to intervene in secular affairs. Serious conflicts not infrequently occurred between them and the civil power; that which raged at Asuncion between the bishop, Bernardino de Cárdenas, and the governor, Gregorio de Hinostrosa, was paralleled in all save its more dramatic features in other provincial capitals. These conflicts were supplemented by quarrels between the episcopate and the officers of the Inquisition, and in Paraguay between the episcopate and the Jesuit Fathers. All these disputes served still further to distract the administration and to produce if not the reality at least the appearance of chaos.

With so many rational grievances, and with such disorders in their government, it is the more surprising that the colonists remained so long under the dominion of Spain and that to Spanish dominion they offered so little opposition. During the three centuries embraced by the colonial period disturbances certainly occurred; towards the close of the period disturbances became somewhat frequent. Yet, when their character is examined, there appears little, if any, indication of a desire to sever the connexion with the mother country. On the contrary, the revolts and seditions which took place are in almost every case attributable to personal or local causes. The exceptions presented by such movements as that led by Gonzalo Pizarro in the early days of Spanish dominion, or that of the communes of Nueva Granada in the latter years of the eighteenth century, were no more than protests against abuses, actual or alleged; the former was directed against the attempted enforcement of the 'New Laws', which would have deprived the settlers of Indian labour, and the latter against burdensome taxation; neither in the one, nor in the other, was there admitted or even concealed disloyalty to the crown. A more political character was assumed by the conspiracy of Berney and Gromuset in Chile, but the vague aspiration towards independence which appears was confined to a few individuals and assuredly did not represent the sentiment of the majority of the population up to the very eve of the outbreak of the wars of independence. It was not until the attempt of Napoleon to place his

brother on the Spanish throne had destroyed all legitimate government in the mother country, that the
separatist movement became in any sense popular.
Until the early years of the nineteenth century Spain
ruled her American possessions with the free consent
and goodwill of their inhabitants.

That consent and goodwill was not the outcome of
gratitude for material benefits received or for intellectual
advantages conferred; it was no tribute to the excellent
organization of the government, and it can hardly be
regarded as the result of fear of the coercive power of
the court of Madrid. It seems, in fact, that the peculiar
administrative system established, a system which was
hardly a system at all, satisfied, during the greater part
of the period for which it endured, the temperament of
the Spanish race and of those who were imbued with
Spanish ideas. In some manner it appealed both to
the inherent love of freedom and also, paradoxical as it
may seem, to the equally inherent love of efficiency,
strengthening both sentiments and resting upon them
for its real support.

IV

THE MAINTENANCE OF THE SPANISH EMPIRE

THAT Spanish dominion in America could not have been so long maintained, had not its continued existence been desired by the great majority of the free population of the colonies, would appear to be incontestable. It is very probable that Charles V or Philip II might have been able to suppress a colonial rebellion and to vindicate their authority by force of arms; it is certain that the accomplishment of such a task would have been entirely beyond the capacity of the last three monarchs of the Austrian dynasty. Under their rule, which occupied the whole of the seventeenth century, Spain was growing constantly more feeble and constantly more impoverished; to administrative disorder and financial distress was added naval and military decline. The valour of the Spanish infantry and the indomitable spirit of the race did for long conceal the reality of weakness and produce an illusion of strength, but even that valour and that spirit would have been unequal to the successful prosecution of arduous campaigns in distant lands, communication with which was always in danger of being interrupted by hostile maritime powers eager to destroy an empire which they regarded with mingled jealousy and fear.

In the succeeding period any coercion of her American possessions would have been not less difficult. During the War of the Spanish Succession, when the mother country was herself the battleground of contending armies, a very wide measure of local autonomy had of necessity to be conceded for the moment to the colonies. That autonomy could have been readily converted into independence had any attempt been made to do so. It is true that the eighteenth century witnessed a considerable revival of Spanish power under the Bourbon kings, but there is little reason to believe that a colonial war could have been waged with any hope of victory. The resources of Spain were hardly adequate to any such undertaking. Even if they had been, the command of the sea save for one brief interlude was continually in the hands of England. An expedition, dispatched to crush an American revolt, could have reached its destination only with the permission of a power most unlikely to accord any such permission.

It was thus not for lack of opportunities to do so that the Spanish provinces in the New World, during the seventeenth and eighteenth centuries, refrained from attempting to sever their connexion with their mother country; the opportunities offered but no effort was made to use them. Had it been made foreign aid would almost certainly have been forthcoming. While at the very zenith of their power, the Dutch endeavoured to form an alliance with the Araucanian Indians and to gain a foothold in Chile, in order to spread disaffection through the provinces of the Pacific coast of South America and thereby to pave the way for the overthrow of Spanish dominion. From the time of Cromwell, when Jamaica was conquered, a similar idea was constantly more or less present in the minds of English statesmen. It is true that the expeditions to which that idea gave birth normally degenerated into little more than mere plundering raids. But they would not have so degenerated had any encouragement been met in the New World; in such circumstances they would rather have developed into serious attempts at conquest as did the expedition against Buenos Aires in the early years of the nineteenth century. No encouragement, however, was received. On the contrary, as the attacks of the Dutch had been repulsed, so those of the English were resisted or defeated by the scanty forces of the colonists themselves.

Such opposition to foreign attack does in itself no more than indicate that the Spanish population preferred the rule of their own compatriots to that of any other nation, since it was not the intention either of the English or of the Dutch to aid in the establishment of independence. In the case of the Dutch, perhaps, it does not even indicate this preference; by their alliance with the Indians, they seriously prejudiced any prospect of success, since they thereby probably roused the colonists to unusual vigour. But it is reasonable to suppose that, if the Spanish possessions had desired the severance of their connexion with Spain, if they had shown any inclination to assert their independence, help both from Holland and from England would have been readily forthcoming. Those two powers did aid Portugal to regain its freedom; at a later date, individual Englishmen contributed not a little to assist the revolt of the Spanish American possessions, and it was the early recognition of the new republics by England that largely served to produce the cessation of efforts on the part of the court of Madrid to recover that which had been lost. It is, indeed, sufficiently clear that it was not by force or by any threat of force, but by goodwill and free consent, that the political union with Spain was so long preserved and that such goodwill and free consent were present despite any prejudicial effect which the union had upon the colonies and despite any vices by which the Spanish colonial administration was characterized.

An explanation of this apparently peculiar fact has been sought in the vast influence exerted in the New World by the Catholic Church. The influence of the Church has almost always been on the side of constituted authority; that it should be so in Spanish America was perhaps inevitable. The rigid orthodoxy of the government was in itself a passport to clerical favour and this passport was the more sure because every effort was made to exclude from the New World any individuals who were even slightly tainted with the suspicion of heresy and any ideas which might be regarded as heretical. Patronage was carefully retained in the hands of the crown; the bishops in America were so many royal agents, pledged beforehand to adhere to that power to which they owed their position. The lower clergy, controlled by their ecclesiastical superiors, were equally so pledged, and perhaps the more so because only in royal favour could they find any hope of substantial preferment. In support of Spanish authority was more especially enlisted the Society of Jesus, despite all those accusations of actual or meditated treason brought against the Fathers at the time of their expulsion. The Jesuits were exempt from episcopal control and between them and the hierarchy conflicts were by no means infrequent. In the province of Paraguay, the bishops of Asunción were their almost inveterate enemies, and the hostility with which they were thus pursued was experienced also from the secular authorities, who yearned to appropriate the vast wealth which the Fathers were credited with having accumulated in their missions. It was no more than natural that the Jesuits should be advocates not merely of the Spanish connexion, but of the direct control of the colonies by the crown, potential enemies not merely of independence, but even of the possession of any wide measure of local autonomy by the civil authorities of the various provinces.

Of the influence exerted by the Church there can certainly be no doubt. Religious by temperament and orthodox by tradition and training, the Spanish race was in general loyal to the creed which it professed, and habitually inclined to defer to the authorized exponents of that creed. In the New World this loyalty was perhaps deepened. From Spanish America heretics were legally excluded; when they did appear there it was generally as enemies and plunderers. Converted Jews and their immediate descendants, and such as had been 'reconciled' by the Inquisition, were forbidden to enter the colonies, a prohibition strongly approved by the colonists themselves, who complained bitterly of the presence of Portuguese Jews from Brazil in Peru during the period of the union of Portugal with Spain. In the early days of the conquest, moreover, placed as they were among a native population in a state of heathendom, every Spaniard felt himself to be something of a crusader and something of a missionary. The solicitude displayed by Pizarro for the conversion of Atahualpa was no pretence; it was an exhibition of that anxiety for the spiritual welfare of the Indians by which all the *conquistadores* were inspired and which was not the less sincere because at times it existed side by side with a somewhat cynical indifference to the material well-being of the natives. During this period, also, the Spaniards were constantly taking their lives in their hands. In face of imminent death they had a special need for the consolations of religion, and they felt themselves to be in a very marked degree dependent upon divine favour and protection. Everything contributed to strengthen their devotion to the Church, and when the actual task of conquest was completed that devotion did not sensibly diminish. It is a significant fact that in Spanish America the efforts of the Inquisition were directed rather to the coercion of recalcitrant clergy than to the extirpation of heresy among the laity, and that of the laymen consigned to its prisons, a very large number were aliens who had evaded the restrictions upon immigration or who had been captured while attempting some act of war, piracy or smuggling against the colonies, and whose offence was rather economic than religious.

The influence of the Church, moreover, was not confined to the creoles and *mestizos*, but extended to

an equal degree over the Indians. The work of conversion was sincerely undertaken and attended with
very great success. It is, indeed, obvious that of those
who embraced Christianity during the period of the
conquest, very many can have had little enough conception of the creed which they adopted. Las Casas com-
plains that the gospel was perfunctorily preached to
the natives in a language which they did not understand.
Such almost miraculous achievements as that of Father
Francisco de Bobadilla, who in nine days converted and
baptized 29,063 Indians in Nicaragua, were discounted
even by contemporaries. It may also be admitted that
as long as Spanish rule endured, individual parish
priests abused their position, exploiting to their own
pecuniary advantage that superstitious terror with
which they inspired the natives. From the *Noticias
Secretas* of Juan and Ulloa, a confidential report on the
colonies prepared by order of Ferdinand VI and presented to Charles III, an impression would be gathered
that the treatment of the Indians by the clergy was
generally shameful, but any such impression would be
erroneous. In the majority of cases sincere service
was rendered by the priesthood; the corruption of a
few does no more than throw into greater relief the
integrity of the many. From the moment when the
work of conversion was entrusted to the Jesuits it was
conducted with all that zeal and devotion for which
the Society has always been renowned. The success
which attended the missionary labours of the Fathers
in the country of the Mainas, until it was brought to a
close by Portuguese attacks, and the still more remarkable success of the missions in Paraguay, are sufficient
evidence that there was no lack either of effort or of
result. The Church was rewarded by the enthusiastic
loyalty of those who were converted, and Catholicism
was so firmly rooted in Spanish America among the
natives, no less than among the non-natives, that in

the present republics, under a régime of complete religious toleration, neither Protestantism, in any of its various forms, nor agnosticism has been able to secure any substantial measure of adhesion.

Since all instruction was in the hands of the Church, and since the character of that instruction was admittedly such as to induce acceptance of the existing order, rather than opposition to it, the share of the Church in preserving Spanish dominion would appear to have been necessarily great. Colour is lent to the suggestion that this share was really paramount by the fact that it is to the second half of the eighteenth century that the first beginnings of the movement by which that dominion was eventually overthrown may be traced. For it was in the second half of the eighteenth century also that the Jesuits were expelled. It was then that the somewhat anticlerical attitude adopted by Charles III permitted the readier propagation of freethinking ideas in his dominions. And it is thus a plausible enough suggestion that the resultant weakening of the influence of the Church undermined the very foundations of Spanish power in the New World.

While, however, it is probable enough that anything which served to facilitate the spread of novel opinions served also to promote criticism of the existing order and criticism which would tend to seek expression in action, the suggestion that the maintenance of the connexion with Spain was mainly the result of the influence of the Church can hardly be substantiated. Despite that orthodoxy of belief by which they have been characterized, the Spanish people, from the Middle Ages onwards, have been little inclined to permit clerical domination in the political sphere. No states so strenuously resisted papal interference as did medieval Castile and Aragon. In the Cortes of the former country the clergy had no regular position; over the municipalities they had no control. Ferdinand

and Isabella themselves, upon whom the title *los Reyes Católicos* was conferred, set an example of independence; they threatened to break off diplomatic relations with Rome when Sixtus IV attempted to impose his nominee upon the see of Cuenca. The army of Charles V sacked Rome; that of Philip II was dispatched to compel the pope to conform his political attitude to that of the Spanish king. In the case of the sack of Rome some indignation was aroused in Spain, but it was due rather to the excesses of the German *lanzknechts* than to the mere fact that Spanish forces had been used to coerce the Papacy. In the other instances there is no indication that royal action was anything but in accord with public opinion. The Society of Jesus was charged with attempting to intervene in secular affairs and its members were expelled. Madrid, which had risen in revolt when Charles III proposed to improve the lighting of the streets and to check an epidemic of assassination by forbidding the wearing of long cloaks under which daggers could be readily concealed, remained calmly indifferent to the fate of the Jesuits.

No greater willingness to accept clerical direction in secular affairs was found in Spanish America. In the frequent conflicts which occurred between the civil and the ecclesiastical authorities popular sympathy was most often on the side of the former; attempted episcopal usurpation of the governors was resented. When Bernardino de Cárdenas attempted to secure control of the government of Paraguay he failed to win the adhesion of the majority of the population, despite the fact that he aspired to a reputation for unusual sanctity and was certainly gifted with some sense of the value of a dramatic appeal. The women of Asunción wept and exalted their bishop to the skies when he stripped to the waist and publicly scourged himself before the high altar of his cathedral, but this did not

enable him to triumph over the governor. In the province of Nueva Granada the disputes which occurred
between the civil and spiritual powers generally found
popular opinion on the side of the former; such exceptions as that presented in the case of the quarrel
between archbishop Bernardino de Almansa and the
marqués de Sofraga were due to excessive unreason-
ableness on the part of the lay authority.

It might, moreover, be reasonably supposed that if
the Church had been the great bulwark of the Spanish
connexion, its influence would have been exerted in
favour of the maintenance of that connexion when the
movement for its dissolution began. But it was not so
exerted. Training and temperament doubtless induced
a number of individual ecclesiastics, as they induced a
number of individual laymen, to support the existing
order; it was impossible that the Church should declare
herself officially in favour of revolution. At the same
time there was no pronounced hostility on the part of
the clergy as a body to the liberation of Spanish America.
They acquiesced with little or no reluctance in the
establishment of a new régime, and they gave to
the republican governments that loyal adhesion which
the Catholic Church habitually accords to a *de facto*,
no less than to a *de iure*, government. Evidence of
the absence of serious opposition to the advocates of
independence is supplied by the relations established
between the civil and ecclesiastical powers in the republics. Religious toleration was, indeed, everywhere
proclaimed, but it was rather in deference to political
theory than to any popular desire. The leaders of the
war of independence were neither heretics nor agnostics,
but Catholics who lived and died in the faith. And
while Catholicism is nowhere an officially established
religion, it is and has been the creed of the overwhelming majority of Spanish Americans. For practical
purposes the severance of political ties with Spain pro-

duced no adverse change in the position of the Church, which was not penalized as it would almost inevitably have been if to the Church Spain had primarily owed her continued dominion.

Of the endurance of that dominion, an alternative explanation has been sought in the suggestion that political life was so stagnant that the existing order lasted for lack of any ability to criticize it and of any desire for a more active political existence. It is true that education was strictly controlled and its scope limited; legally the free circulation and discussion of ideas was hardly possible. Communication with the outside world was greatly impeded, and to some extent at least, during the greater part of the colonial period, political thought was officially cramped. It is equally true that, prior to the outbreak of the war of independence, various factors had contributed to bring new ideas to the attention of the colonists and to produce a considerable discussion of those ideas. From the beginning of the eighteenth century, as a result of the development of illicit or of quasi-illicit trade, some knowledge of English institutions and later of French political thought was diffused through Spanish America. The liberalism of Charles III permitted the spread to Spain of the speculations of contemporary free-thinkers; from Spáin those speculations passed to her provinces in the New World, and were there rendered the more attractive and the more influential by being garbed in a Spanish dress. The production of books in the colonies themselves increased; while the censorship was nominally maintained in full vigour, actually its operation became far less effective. Spanish America was further affected by the establishment of the independence of the United States. An example of the successful assertion by colonists of the right to govern themselves was thereby afforded; the assertion of that right had been officially supported by the court of

Madrid and hence royal approval was apparently given
to the principle involved. The French Revolution, and
more especially the crystallization of somewhat vague
conceptions in telling phrases, was an additional factor
tending to arouse political debate. There is thus no
little plausibility in the suggestion that the movement
against Spanish dominion was originally delayed by the
stagnation of political life and that it became active as
soon as that stagnation was brought to an end.

The suggestion is, however, rather plausible than
true, since the political stagnation was rather apparent
than real. The creoles were certainly excluded for the
most part from all high offices; the central administration was in the hands mainly of individuals sent out
from Spain. It is not therefore true that political life
in the colonies was dead or even stagnant. The supposition that it was either has arisen from a certain
forgetfulness of one of the most marked characteristics
of Spain, of the fact that in Spain local institutions
were always far more vital to the people than central
institutions. It was not in the Cortes that the political
life of Castile found its expression. That body did
certainly register protests against misgovernment; it
castigated abuses and petitioned for reforms; it granted
some supplies and in it laws were promulgated. But it
was never representative of the nation. It was not an
assembly of estates, for the membership in it of the
nobles and clergy was uncertain and irregular. It was
not a gathering of the deputies of the commons, for
no more than a limited number of cities and towns
ever had the right to send proctors to it and that right
was, at a comparatively early date, confined to seventeen
selected places. It was essentially a privileged, not a
popular, body, and upon the affection and trust of the
people it had no great hold. It is significant that
while it was rarely summoned to meet by Ferdinand
and Isabella, when autocracy was in process of develop-

ment, it was frequently convoked by Philip II, when autocracy was at its very zenith, so readily did it become a convenient agency for the registration of the royal will. The complete subordination of the Cortes to the crown aroused no general resistance; it led to no revolt, to no riot. There is hardly evidence that it gave cause even to sentimental regret.

There was little reason why it should, for the political life of Castile was lived not in the Cortes, but in the municipalities. From the earliest times, the cities and towns enjoyed a wide measure of self-government; the *cabildos*, municipal councils, were popular bodies, elected by the people and acting in their name. Membership of them was eagerly sought; intense feeling was aroused when elections occurred and the conflict of parties within the municipalities was always lively and not infrequently riotous. Indeed, so violent were the disputes that they afforded a plausible excuse for the gradual suppression of municipal liberty by the crown; Ferdinand and Isabella made them the ground for the substitution of nomination for election at Cáceres and at other places, and royal officials, appointed to preserve or to restore public order, eventually usurped the functions originally exercised by popularly chosen magistrates. The change was bitterly resented. Protests were addressed to Ferdinand and Isabella; the right of the cities and towns to govern themselves was vigorously asserted. The protests were ignored by the crown; the right was implicitly denied and actually abrogated. In the early years of Charles V, action took the place of mere words; the revolt of the *comuneros* was an attempt to regain municipal independence and to preserve the political life of Castile from extinction or suspension.

It is a fact of supreme importance in the history of Spanish America that the period during which the municipal liberties of Castile were in process of destruc-

tion was also the period during which the empire of
Spain in the New World was in process of formation
and organization. Those who crossed the Atlantic
carried with them that ardent love of local self-government, expression of which in Spain was becoming
increasingly difficult, and when they began the coloniza-
tion of America, they did not forget the old municipal
life of Castile. Every settlement which they founded
was organized upon the traditional Castilian model;
a *cabildo* was created, its members being indeed originally nominated by the founder, but being subsequently
elected by the inhabitants. The home government,
in pursuance of its idea of establishing a system of
checks and balances, not only permitted but enjoined
this practice; the Laws of the Indies prescribed
that such should be the organization of every colonial
town.

In these municipalities there was no stagnation;
political life was always robust and active. That independence, which had been so prized in Spain and for
which the *comuneros* had fought, was jealously guarded
in Spanish America. The remoter settlements had of
necessity to be permitted to direct their own affairs;
external interference was rendered almost impossible
by difficulty of communication. It was moreover inadvisable to attempt any complete limitation of freedom
of action; as the towns of medieval Castile had been
allowed to rule themselves because they were required
also to defend themselves against Moorish attack, so
the towns of many parts of Spanish America were
allowed to direct their own affairs because they were
exposed to attack by the surrounding Indians. How
necessary such independence was for the safety of the
settlements was illustrated in the province of Tucumán,
where Cañete, Londres and Córdoba were overwhelmed
partly because two conflicting authorities were attempting to control them.

Even in the very seats of the central government the *cabildos* constantly asserted their freedom, resisting attempted dictation whether by viceroys, governors or *audiencias*. Nothing could, indeed, be more untrue than the suggestion which has been made that municipal life in Spanish America was *una sombra de una sombra*, the shadow of an unreality. On the contrary, that life was real; in the colonies, as had formerly been the case in the mother country, it was in the towns that the political activity of the race found expression. The central administration may have been stagnant; local administration was not, and it is, after all, in the vitality of local institutions, far more than in that of central institutions, that the true political life of a people is found.

A population, so politically active, needed no foreign tuition in order to conceive of change in the existing order. It cannot have been incapable of any such conception, for in the management of local affairs it of necessity acquired that experience which impels towards the consideration of possible development. The mere fact that upon the ruins of the Spanish empire republics were organized is proof that in the minds of the colonists political ideas were present and the capacity for translating those ideas into action existent. For the organization of the republics was not the achievement of a handful of eminent individuals; it was by the will and by the effort of the population as a whole that it was accomplished. It would be wholly erroneous to suppose that Spanish Americans followed blindly and without understanding the guidance afforded to them by some few who had been educated in Europe or who had imbibed foreign ideas. So far from being thus led, it is significant that Simon Bolivar himself was unable to impose upon Venezuela that form of government which he personally desired to see established; he was obliged to submit to the will of those who, devoted as

they were to their great leader, were yet not less devoted, at least subconsciously, to their conception of
the true organization of society. Ideas so vigorously
held could not have been acquired in a moment, in a
few years, and least of all so acquired in a period occupied by an arduous and uncertain war. Even if it be
admitted that in some degree these ideas originated outside Spanish America, their adoption by the colonists
still argues a receptivity of mind which could only be
the result of past training, which could not have been
found in men who had never known any active political
life. Had that life really been stagnant men would
have been unable to make any independent choice
between opposing theories of state organization. They
would infallibly have followed a leader whom they
justly admired and respected, in the person of Bolivar,
rather than the guidance of others of less outstanding
personality and with less claim upon their devotion.
Nor, if there had been any real deadness politically
during the colonial period, would the development of the
republics have been so rapid as it has in actual fact been.
So far from a century witnessing the creation of stable
and progressive states, it may be safely conjectured that
Spanish America would to-day be in a condition similar
to that of the states of the Balkan peninsula. To find
in the supposition of political stagnation the explanation
of the long continuance of Spanish dominion is to
entertain a completely fallacious idea; it is even to
suppose the occurrence in Spanish America of a political
miracle without parallel elsewhere in the world. For
it is to imagine a race, long dead to political ideas and
sunk in an ignorant stupor, suddenly acquiring a vigorous
political mentality and a keen appreciation of the
theories of government, coupled with no little ability
to put those theories into practice.

The continuance of Spanish dominion can, in short,
be explained only by the absence of any strong desire to

bring about a change, and the absence of such desire can in turn be explained only by the fact that the colonists, despite the disabilities under which they laboured and the privations which they endured, were really content with the existing order. Whatever may have been its defects, the administrative system established in the American possessions of Spain was one suited to the Spanish race and to those who had acquired the Spanish outlook upon life and upon affairs. It endured so long as it gratified both the innate love of individual liberty and the innate love of efficient government; when it ceased to do so, it was overthrown.

That it should have gratified love of personal and local freedom is in no wise surprising, despite the restraints which were legally imposed upon many activities. The very existence of a system of checks and balances ensured that no official should possess power seriously to interfere with the ordinary life of an individual or of a district. The governors and the *audiencias* were normally beyond the effective control of the viceroys; the *cabildos* were not dominated by any other authority, and while they were themselves popular bodies, examples of local self-government, they were little able to control the citizens by whom they were chosen; the seditions of Potosi, which required the personal intervention of the viceroy, were only one illustration of the relative impotence of the local magistrates. Any individual who came into conflict with one authority was almost assured beforehand of countenance by some other authority; in all important cases he had the further recourse of appeal to the Council of the Indies, to the Casa or the crown. The very lack of coercive jurisdiction ensured that the law could be constantly disregarded with impunity; the traditional remark of the viceroys on receiving a royal edict, 'I obey but I do not perform', might have been made by almost every free person in Spanish America,

except, perhaps, the Indians. That freedom, which
had been enjoyed in Spain prior to the abrogation of
the *fueros*, was enjoyed by the scattered communities
of the colonies, and the very government which at
home suppressed, in the New World encouraged, the
assertion of local independence. A somewhat curious
contrast can be found between the Spanish and the
English colonies in the New World. In the latter,
founded by those who had left a country of free institutions in search of still greater freedom, the 'Blue Laws'
were created and a man is alleged to have been put
to death for the crime of kissing his wife publicly
on a Sunday. In the former, established by the subjects of a despotic government and organized by that
government, a greater measure of personal liberty
was permitted to the inhabitants than was enjoyed
at that time by the people of any other country in
the world.

In view of the non-enforcement of law, of the
inability of constituted authority to compel obedience
to its orders, it may seem that to suggest that Spanish
love of efficient government was also fully gratified in
the colonies, is the veriest absurdity. But the paradox
is not the less true. It has always been characteristic
of the Spaniard to desire that a ruler should rule; it
is part of his very idealism, which impels him to believe
that whatever a man finds to do, he should do it with
his might. In theory, this desire was gratified to the
very fullest extent in Spanish America. Almost every
detail of life was legally regulated. The government
professed to decide what the colonists should be taught
and how, what they should read, what they should
discuss, what they should believe. It determined what
goods might be imported and how and where, and in
what manner their distribution should be effected. It
permitted certain forms of production in the colonies
and prohibited others. The government took into its

care the most intimate relationships of private life and the most trivial matters; it claimed to direct the matrimonial affairs of its subjects; it descended to forbid the natives to indulge their fondness for frequent and injudicious bathing. So far as theory and law went, there was no lack of rule. The administrative system was the very apotheosis of paternal despotism and as such was altogether in accord with the Spanish belief that it is the primary function of a government to govern.

The fact was, indeed, very different from the theory; the innumerable laws and regulations were very largely a dead letter. For that very reason they were the more suited to the Spanish temperament. For while every Spaniard wished the ruler to rule, he wished not less that an exception should be made in his own individual case; he would be free himself to do as he pleased, while he would have all others directed from above. Such was the exact condition apparently produced in Spanish America. Each individual knew that, as an actual matter of fact, he was in general as free as he desired to be. He could produce commodities of which the production was prohibited; he could procure from smugglers goods which he was forbidden to receive save through certain authorized channels or which he was forbidden to receive at all. He could obtain and read proscribed literature; he could express opinions which were officially anathematized, and even the most despotic government cannot control the thoughts of its subjects. At the same time, he knew that all this liberty was denied by the ruler who fulfilled his function by restricting freedom within the narrowest limits. It is the quality of an idealist generally to believe to be true that which he hopes and wishes to be true, and the Spaniards are a most idealistic race. The inhabitants of the American possessions of Spain wished the government to put into practice the theories which it proclaimed; they wished the ruler to rule, and it was not difficult for them to believe that their wishes were realized. The perfect reconciliation of two incompatibles was thus seemingly attained; individual freedom was little restricted and government was complete and therefore efficient.

The belief that this had been achieved was not a little facilitated by the concentration of all ultimate power in the hands of the crown. For if it were often only too evident that the holders of immediate authority in the New World were unable to enforce that authority, and that hence the viceroys and governors did not in reality fulfil their nominal functions, it was a consolatory reflection to a race, believing in efficient government, that with these officials the supreme decision was not even theoretically supposed to lie. It was easy enough to attain the conviction that the orders of the king, who was supreme, were invariably carried out, and the more so because there was no one who did not profess his ready and implicit obedience to every royal command. The divergence between professions and actions was thus simply explained; it was denied that any such divergence existed. If an edict, promulgated by the authorities in America, were flagrantly violated, it was asserted, and was perhaps really believed, that the edict did not in truth emanate from the crown and that the royal will had been misrepresented; disobedience became, in fact, the truest obedience. Some such contention was actually advanced by those who resisted the enforcement of the 'New Laws', by which the settlers would have been deprived of native labour, and to that contention a certain colour was lent by the early abrogation or suspension of those laws by Charles V. The theory that to ignore an edict was to obey the king received not infrequent justification from the fact that those who resisted the commands of the authorities in America were as often as not supported, and their action approved by the authorities in Spain. The court of Madrid, indeed, seemed constantly to anticipate the elder Pitt and to 'rejoice that America had resisted'.

Defective as the Spanish system of government in the New World was, when judged by any ordinary standards, it was thus not defective in the eyes of those who were primarily concerned. Despite the constant complaints made against it, it satisfied the colonists, and the degree to which it did so may be possibly gauged from the curious fact that the reformation of that system, the modification of those characteristics in it which seemed to be most pernicious, was almost immediately followed by the War of Independence. In the interests of an efficient government the original viceroyalties were partitioned; in the interests of economic development the restraints upon trade and industry were relaxed. A far greater measure of legal freedom was conceded, and was united with an attempt to enforce such laws as were retained more effectually. A tendency appeared to admit creoles to the higher offices in the administration, and finally deputies from the colonies were summoned to the Cortes in Spain, and the colonists were officially informed that in future they would govern themselves. That system which had prevailed for close upon three hundred years was in process of reversal when the first movements towards independence occurred. It had a somewhat curious illustration of the irony of history that Charles III, the most enlightened and liberally-minded of rulers, by his very best effort to remove those abuses, the existence of which seemed to threaten the dissolution of his empire, did perhaps more than any other one individual to make that dissolution inevitable. He was the Diocletian of Spain. As Diocletian by breaking away from the old traditions of the Roman Empire gave it apparently a new lease of life and yet in fact hurried on its fall, so Charles III, attempting to re-organize his dominions upon a new basis, destroyed in its system of government those very characteristics which had enabled Spanish dominion in the New World to be so long maintained. He was the true author of the War of Independence.

V

THE POPULAR CONCEPTION OF THE WAR OF INDEPENDENCE

WITH some apparent justice the War of Independence has been represented as the almost inevitable outcome of the disadvantages which union with Spain entailed upon her American possessions. Those disadvantages existed from the very first, but were not fully realized until towards the close of the eighteenth century, despite the fact that, as early as the second half of the sixteenth century, the viceroys complained that the creoles were disaffected. In some measure they were the natural outcome of the fundamental theory that the overseas dominions of the Spanish crown were not colonies, but the personal property of the sovereign. Their inhabitants accordingly laboured under certain disabilities which were the lot of all who lived in the remoter districts of a highly centralized country, where communications were imperfect. In Spain itself those areas which were remote from the centre of government were inevitably prejudiced by the concentration of power in the hands of the authorities at Madrid, who were little in touch with local life and local conditions and were hence little in sympathy with local aspirations. The restlessness of Galicia or of the Basque provinces may to some extent be attributed to such imperfection of contact.

In the case of the New World that imperfection was obviously greater. Those responsible for drawing up regulations for the Indies were more often than not personally unacquainted with the lands for which they legislated; the famous 'New Laws' would never have been issued if the advisers of Charles V had possessed first-hand knowledge of America and of the natives. Many edicts, excellent in their intention, were vitiated by the fact that they were framed by men ignorant of the conditions with which they had to deal and thus easily misled by importunate advocates of impossible reforms. The success attained by Las Casas in Spain was due to the defective information possessed by members of the royal council; the idealism of the Spanish race made the task of the 'Apostle of the Indies' relatively easy and facilitated the promulgation of laws which, had they been enforced, would have involved the speedy extinction of Spanish dominion in the New World.

It followed also, as a corollary of the doctrine that Spanish America was as integral a part of Spain as Andalusia or Murcia, that its inhabitants should have no more voice in the control of their own affairs than was accorded to the inhabitants of any province of the peninsula. The creoles were regarded as having no more claim to be entrusted with the work of governing Spanish America than the Gallegos had to be entrusted with the government of Galicia, no more right to be consulted concerning the terms of edicts issued for the regulation of their life. It was as legitimate to impose restraints upon them as upon the inhabitants of Leon or Estremadura, to subordinate their interests to those of Spain as a whole and to use their resources primarily for the purposes of the mother country.

At first, however, this conception of the relations between Spain and her American possessions entailed no serious consequences and was not seriously resented. Those laws which would have produced an impossible economic situation were not enforced; the more grievous were suspended or abrogated. A considerable proportion of those who went to the New World did so with the intention of returning to Europe and they were thus little interested in the administrative methods which might be adopted in a land in which they were only residing for a time. The restraints imposed on settlers in the early days of Spanish dominion were not wholly irrational. There was some justification for insisting that the attention of Spaniards in America should be, as far as possible, concentrated upon the task of exploration, conquest and pacification, upon the introduction of the creed and culture of the mother country, upon the consolidation of possession. The passion for discovery and that crusading spirit by which the *conquistadores* were inspired would in any event have probably led to such concentration; that the authorities in Spain should demand it was wholly in accord with the sentiments of those most nearly concerned. It was, moreover, of little moment to the companions of Cortés or a Pizarro, that they should be forbidden to produce many commodities of which they stood in need, since such production, even if it had been freely permitted, would hardly have been possible. That attention should be especially devoted to the exploitation of gold and silver mines appeared to be reasonable enough in the eyes of men who were convinced that the precious metals alone constituted wealth. It was to them the more reasonable since they were also convinced that the Spanish crown had a moral, and even a religious, right to exact contributions from its American possessions. Agriculture, the pursuit of which was essential for the supply of necessary foodstuffs, was both permitted and enjoined by the home government, more particularly in such areas as were found to be poor in gold and silver. The raising of stock in Tucumán especially was encouraged. In general, the regulations drawn up by the Casa de Contratación weighed lightly enough upon the colonies in their infancy.

But with the establishment of a more settled order those regulations became increasingly irksome, despite the fact that they were persistently violated. Their variety and scope was extended, as, in the opinion of the authorities in Spain, it became necessary to forbid the inhabitants of the New World to engage in activi-

ties, the pursuit of which they had not originally contemplated. Their burdensome character was more and
more fully realized. The potential resources of America
were better understood and the ambition to develop
those resources became more general. The needs and
the desires of a growing population became more
diverse; their satisfaction, under the existing system,
became more difficult. Many creoles visited Europe
and returned with changed economic ideas; those ideas
gained ground in the New World and the more readily
because the production of gold and silver declined as
time went on; placer mining was the system generally
used in Spanish America and placer mining becomes
invariably less profitable the longer it is practised. A
dissatisfaction, which had once been hardly felt, became
more intense with each succeeding generation.

Still greater dissatisfaction was eventually caused by
the exclusion of the creoles from all high office. So
long as the number of those born in America of pure
Spanish blood was small, their exclusion was neither
very important nor much regarded. But the ranks of
the excluded were constantly recruited, until a grievance
which had been felt only by a few was felt by very
many. It was the more felt because the forms of
occupation in which the creoles found it possible to
engage were somewhat limited in number. The most
fortunate held landed property and achieved opulence
from the cultivation of an amazingly fertile soil by
native labour. Some were absorbed in the rather
scanty naval and military establishments, although
here high command was normally obtainable only by
chapetones, Spaniards who had been born in Spain.
Many entered the Church; at an early date, it was
found necessary to limit the number of those who
should be allowed to embrace a celibate life, since in
a new, no less than in a declining, state 'the virtues of
the clergy are more dangerous than their vices'. They

filled the learned professions; so numerous were the
lawyers that they became a source of grave anxiety to
a paternally minded government, desirous of restraining
within reasonable bounds that passion for litigation
which was innate in the Spanish, and which had been
only too readily acquired by the Indian race. Some
established factories, despite legal prohibitions; some
were receivers and distributors of contraband goods.
But very many were left without occupation, since all
subordinate positions were left to the *mestizos* and
all manual labour to the natives or to negroes. The
unemployed creoles lived a precarious existence, trusting
either to the careless bounty of some wealthy patron
or to the arts of a Guzman de Alfarache. To rich and
poor alike, exclusion from government employment was
a source of extreme irritation. Those who were wealthy
felt themselves to be entitled to high position in the
royal service for that very reason. Those who were
relatively or actually in a condition of poverty were
assured that if a career in that service were thrown open
to them, their necessities would be speedily relieved, even
if their official salaries were inadequate and unpaid.

The creoles had here sufficient ground for complaint,
but their complaining would have been less bitter if it
had been no more than a question of exclusion from a
probably profitable form of occupation. The Spaniard
has always been far more ready to suffer material
distress than to endure anything which even seems to
imply social degradation. Habitually courteous by
temperament he demands courtesy from others; the
very deference which he is ready to accord to birth and
rank is the proud deference rendered by a man who
feels that he is himself by nature a *caballero*. It is
almost true to say that, in Spain, the inferiority complex
is unknown save to those who have become un-Spanish
in their outlook upon life. Respect is yielded because
respect is demanded in return; the Spaniard respects

others because he first respects himself. The creoles undoubtedly resented their exclusion from employment upon material grounds; they resented it far more upon social grounds. The 'Europeans', the *chapetones*, inclined to treat them with a haughty contempt, which was as galling as it was unjustifiable; implicitly, if not explicitly, they declared those born in the New World to be of inferior status. The claim of the creoles to purity of descent was at least covertly derided; it was received with a sneer peculiarly offensive to a sensitive race, by which a distinguished ancestry has always been very highly prized.

The effect of such social discrimination on the part of the 'Europeans' against the creoles was important; it resulted in an alliance between those of pure Spanish blood and the *mestizos*. These two sections of the population had been long divided, but the barrier between them was gradually broken down and was broken down the more easily because its original erection was not due to that hatred for the mixed blood which is so characteristic of the Teutonic races. In Spain itself alliances between Castilians and Moors had been frequent; during the Middle Ages, intermarriage was common and one Aragonese princess actually became the principal wife of a Mohammedan emir. In America unions between the settlers and the natives had been encouraged by repeated royal *cédulas*; an ordinance of Ferdinand and Isabella granted letters of nobility to any Castilian who married the daughter of a cacique, and in another ordinance the same sovereigns urged marriage between Castilian women and Indians. The fact that very many of the settlers were unmarried or had left their wives in Spain, coupled with the fact that the emigration of unmarried women to the Indies was so restricted as to be almost forbidden, resulted in a very considerable admixture of blood.

It was not any feeling of repulsion based upon the ground of colour which led the creoles to hold themselves somewhat aloof from the *mestizos*. The explanation of their attitude is to be sought elsewhere. The origin of the majority of those of mixed blood was traceable to illicit unions and religious feeling on the subject of illegitimacy prejudiced their position; even when illegitimacy could not be proved, it was almost invariably suspected. The perfectly sincere efforts of the Spanish government, moreover, to establish equality between the two races in the New World were really foredoomed to failure. The virile Castilian could and did respect the equally virile Araucanian; he regarded with some contempt the feeble inhabitants of some of the islands or of Peru, and he regarded with horror the savages whom he found in other islands and in some districts of the mainland. He was disposed to find in the effeminacy of the one type and in the brutality of the other, proof of a degraded nature; he was not entirely convinced that either the tame or the wild Indians could be classed as human beings. The stigma of inferiority was further affixed to the natives by the fact that to them were assigned those menial and quasi-servile functions which the Spaniard refused to perform; upon occupational, rather than upon sociological, grounds, the Indians were despised. This contempt was not unnaturally shared by those in whose veins native blood was known or was supposed to flow. There was, perhaps, a half unconscious desire to reduce the *mestizo* to the Indian level, in order thereby to supply that lack of labour which resulted from the decline of the native population in many districts. It may be added that the claim of many *mestizos* to be *mestizos* was disputed, and with some justification since pure blooded Indians were often in the habit of asserting themselves to be of partly Spanish descent in order to escape in this way from compulsory labour.

But as the barrier between the two sections of the population was thus not the result of any fundamental cause, it was readily broken down in face of a common grievance; the *chapetones* found themselves in opposition to the united forces of the creoles and the *mestizos*. In the course of the eighteenth century, a new society came into being, and the continuance of a régime, which had rested very largely upon the divisions in the free population of the colonies, was at once imperilled. It was imperilled still further by a certain reconciliation between the Spanish and quasi-Spanish sections and the natives, the result of the impossibility of drawing any clear line between the almost entirely Indian *mestizo* and the pure Indian, and of the philanthropic ideas of the period, which popularized the conception of the 'noble savage'.

This new society speedily realized its strength and began to claim with ever greater insistence freedom to determine its own fate. In doing so it was in accord with the prevalent sentiment of the age. Even a Frederic the Great had declared himself to be the first servant of his people, and that government should be for the good of the governed was an axiom to all who lived in an age of enlightened despotism. The example afforded by the United States suggested the legitimate remedy which might be applied, if a ruler failed to perform his recognized duty; it asserted the right and illustrated the capacity of colonists to establish their own independence and to determine their own form of government. That example was fortified by the teaching of French political writers and by the occurrence of the French Revolution. Almost immediately afterwards, a situation was produced which seemed to make continued loyalty impossible and which certainly rendered doubtful the object of allegiance. The overthrow of the Bourbons by Napoleon and the attempted imposition of Joseph

Bonaparte upon Spain resulted in the appearance of various claimants to the obedience of the colonies; that obedience was demanded by agents of Charles IV, of Ferdinand VII, of Joseph, and of the Supreme Junta. To refuse allegiance in such circumstances might appear to be reasonable enough; to make terms upon which it would be yielded to be still more reasonable. Those who aspired to effect changes in the existing system of administration and those who dreamed vaguely of complete independence alike found their hands immeasurably strengthened by the anarchy which prevailed in the mother country. The movement for the dissolution of the Spanish connexion, the result of accumulated abuses and the ultimate outcome of an unrest which had been growing all through the eighteenth century, took definite shape at the moment when the necessary opportunity was supplied, when the political ideas of the colonists had attained sufficient development, when the forces of resistance had been consolidated and when the home government was in no position to crush revolution in its infancy.

The revolutionary movement has thus been regarded as in great measure the product of the North American War of Independence and of the French Revolution; it has at the same time been represented as being both anti-Spanish and non-Spanish in its character and its aims. It was the outcome of that system of government which Spain had created and maintained. The colonists had once hoped for reforms; as early as the reign of Philip V, the more enlightened of the creoles had urged that they should be admitted to high office. Their hopes had been disappointed. The sluggish conservatism of the court of Madrid effectually prevented the taking of those steps which might have removed the grievances of Spanish America and prepared the way for the establishment of an enduring harmony. Such half tentative measures as were adopted by the more liberal governments of Ferdinand VI and Charles III failed to go to the root of the matter; the prejudiced position of the creoles was unchanged. Even such good as was effected was very largely undone by the reactionary principles professed by Charles IV or by the advisers of that incompetent monarch. Advance was stayed, and this was the more disastrous for Spain because it falsified expectations which had been aroused, because it coincided with the awakening of political life in the colonies, and with that trumpet-call to liberty which was sounded by the fall of the Bastille. Not merely a few, but the vast majority, of the free inhabitants of Spanish America became convinced that from Madrid no good thing could come, and that, if they would improve their lot, it was necessary to follow the example so brilliantly set by the English colonists in North America. Spain had been weighed in the balance and found wanting. She had been given for nearly three centuries the opportunity to set the world an example in the organization of overseas possessions, but she had failed to take that opportunity and now it had passed for ever. To end Spanish dominion was the first and foremost aim of the leaders of the united creoles and *mestizos*.

As the movement was anti-Spanish, so it was non-Spanish in character. In the conceptions of those who proclaimed the War of Independence there was nothing of those ideas by which Spain had always been most influenced. Devotion to orthodoxy of religious faith, championship of an intensely national culture, were replaced by the idea of religious toleration, by a cosmopolitanism which almost derided patriotism. The opinions professed by the revolutionary leaders were born not south, but north, of the Pyrenees; they originated from Locke and Montesquieu and Rousseau: their inspiration was derived from London or Paris, whence they had, perhaps, travelled by way of Philadelphia and Washington. Liberty and equality, ideas alien to a country which had for centuries been autocratically governed and in which distinctions of class were almost rooted in the soil; fraternity, an idea not less alien to a people who could approve the Inquisition and who had gloried in the expulsion of the Jews and the Moriscoes, were the ideas which filled the minds of the colonists as they entered upon the struggle for independence. They declared themselves to be the champions of the long oppressed Indians and the liberators of the enslaved Africans, thereby breaking away effectually from all the practice of their Spanish rulers during the colonial period. They proclaimed the adoption of representative institutions, the typically Anglo-Saxon form of government, a system in which Spain had never really shared even in the days of her medieval freedom. The conception of equal justice and of equality of taxation was also non-Spanish; neither had been known in a land in which at first law varied from district to district and where later justice was almost notoriously partial and corrupt, where an iniquitous financial system had survived even the attack upon it of an enlightened and autocratic king. The movement was, in short, Anglo-French or Franco-North American; it was emphatically not Spanish.

While, however, there is much truth in the suggestion that the grievances of the colonists were more acutely felt in the eighteenth century than they had been at an earlier date and in the description of the professed aims of the leaders of the revolution, the resultant conception of the character of the war of independence is at best only partially accurate. It is clear that upon *a priori* grounds, its accuracy is open to question. It is certain enough that the basis of the civilization of Spanish America prior to the dissolution of the union with Spain was, as it is to-day, Spanish; that the leaders of the movement for independence were Spaniards, and that their

political ideas, whatever may have been the ultimate
origin of those ideas, were acquired by them mainly
in Spain or through Spanish sources. It is more than
probable that in any other circumstances they would
have been far less receptive of the theories which they
adopted; it is even more probable that they would have
failed to secure for those theories any wide acceptance
in America. Spain has always been intensely patriotic
in the sense that she has never been willing to allow her
outlook upon any subject to be approximated to that
of any foreign nation. The Renaissance came early to
the peninsula, but it there assumed a character which
was wholly distinct from that which it assumed in
Italy, in France, in Germany, or in England. The
conception of a reformed Church was familiar in Spain
long before Erasmus laid or Luther hatched the egg
of the Protestant Reformation; Isabella the Catholic
and Ximenes were essentially reformers. But the
Spanish conception was not that of a Church with
modified or changed doctrines, but of a Church wholly
orthodox, though purged of moral abuses. The Society
of Jesus originated in a Spanish mind and embodied
Spanish ideas; Protestantism never gained any real hold
upon the nation, nor would it have done so even if the
government had practised the very widest toleration.
At a time when in almost every European country the
example of Versailles was followed with some approach
to servility, Spain, outside the immediate entourage of
the sovereign, was little affected; the ceremonial of the
court itself remained Spanish, and despite the aphorism
of Louis XIV, the Pyrenees continued to exist and to
present an almost impassable barrier against influences
from the north. The effort of Philip V to approximate
the Spanish to the French nobility called forth a vigorous protest from the duque de Arcos; the establishment of the Bourbon dynasty entirely failed to gallicize
the nation and failed even to gallicize the palace. The

Spanish Americans shared in this national exclusiveness, an exclusiveness born in some measure of a proud conviction of superiority. The race was willing to consider foreign ideas; it was not willing to adopt them until they had been modified to an accord with their own conceptions. The political theories of London and Paris were carried across the Atlantic garbed in their original phraseology, but they were given a meaning which was not that given to them in the lands where they had been first formulated.

When the declarations of those who led the movement are considered it becomes even more obvious that so far from being non-Spanish, that movement was most emphatically Spanish in character. Liberty had always been prized by the race, even during the period during which government was most autocratic; equality was a conception naturally understood by a nation, the humblest member of which was deeply convinced of his right to be treated with respect by the most exalted and in which the prevalent religious creed was that which in practice had always been democratic. To the French, the two phrases, *liberté*, *égalité*, represented abstract ideals, towards the attainment of which little real effort was made even in the heyday of revolutionary ardour; in only one of the various constitutions produced after the beginning of the Revolution was the distinction between 'active' and 'passive' citizens abandoned, and that the constitution was never even temporarily put into operation. To the Spaniards, the two phrases were almost commonplaces, and the fact that they were so was obscured only by the coincident fact that liberty was not regarded as being incompatible with government or equality with the rendering of a freely accorded deference.

Championship of the rights of the Indians was no more than an echo of the regulations of every Spanish sovereign from the days when Ferdinand and Isabella

had proclaimed the natives to be free vassals of the
crown of Castile and had censured and reversed their
enslavement by Columbus. The enthusiastic support
accorded in Spain to Las Casas is proof enough that
such championship was not alien from the Spanish outlook upon life in the first period of the Spanish empire;
that it did not become so may be gathered from the
whole tenour of the *Noticias Secretas*. It is, indeed,
remarkable that the bitterest criticism of the treatment
accorded to the natives came from Spaniards and that
the strongest defence of their conduct came from
foreigners. It was by Spaniards also that the earliest
protests against negro slavery were made. Nicolas de
Ovando requested Ferdinand and Isabella to prohibit
the exportation of Africans to Haiti, and Las Casas
bitterly repented and publicly recanted his original
advocacy of such exportation as a means whereby labour
might be obtained without forcing it upon the Indians.
The idea of representative government, in the form in
which it has been established in most countries of the
world, is English, but the root principle underlying it
can be found in Aragon, and to a lesser degree in Castile,
at a time when England was still organized upon a
wholly different basis. Equality of justice was a conception familiar to a people whose sovereigns were, at least
upon one day in each week, accessible to suitors of
whatever rank or class; equality of taxation to those
who were all similarly required to contribute to the
maintenance of the Santa Hermandad, unless exempted
on the ground of personal service. There is in history
hardly a more striking example of a high conception
of the right of all subjects to receive justice than that
which is afforded by the famous suit brought by Diego
Columbus against Ferdinand the Catholic, a suit the
whole story of which reflects equal credit upon the
absolute monarch who allowed it to be heard and upon
the judges who decided it against the king at whose

pleasure they held their positions. The belief, indeed, that the ideas of the revolutionary leaders were non-Spanish is the result of concentration of attention upon Spain as she was in her decline under the later Habsburg monarchs, to a forgetfulness of Spain as she was at the zenith of her power.

To trace the War of Independence to the events which immediately preceded it, whether in the New World or the Old, is to take a superficial view of the movement, to confound the occasion with the cause. To regard the movement as non-Spanish is to misunderstand both the war itself and the temper of the Spanish race. That movement was, on the contrary, essentially an expression of the deepest feelings of that race, an attempt to realize those ideals which it cherished most dearly and which were derived not from any external sources, but from the very hearts of the people. It was not directed to give expression in action to some ideas recently and no more than superficially acquired from the writings of alien political thinkers, but to attain those ends which had in great measure been attained by the Spanish administration in the New World and which had become less attainable as a result of modifications effected in that system by rulers who, however well-intentioned and enlightened, were not wholly in harmony with the nation which they had been called upon to rule.

As it was a Spanish movement, so it was led by Spaniards and was not in its inception or in its development anti-Spanish. It must be remembered that the king, to whom opposition was eventually offered, was only a Spaniard by adoption and certainly not by grace. The Bourbon dynasty had not attained that sympathy with their people which had been possessed by an Isabella the Catholic or by a Philip II, which is to-day possessed by Alfonso XIII. It was against the un-Spanish attitude of the government that the movement was

directed, and if its leaders advocated dissolution of the
political union with Spain, it was only under a melancholy compulsion, it was only because Spain herself
has ceased to be true to her own ideals, because into
the administration of the colonies there had been
intruded ideas which were foreign. In the War of
Independence, creoles fought upon both sides; in some,
love for Spain still refused to believe any evil; in others,
who were convinced of the evil, the very conviction was
a sorrow. Bolivar himself, probably the greatest of all
the leaders, was great because he was so Spanish, because
he so fully represented Spanish ideas, because he so
fully appreciated that the war in Venezuela was fought
not by Venezuelans against Spaniards, but by Venezuelans against Venezuelans, by Spaniards against
Spaniards. He understood the attitude of his opponents and accorded to them that respect which was
due to honest difference of opinion, as the elder Pitt
understood that the American colonists were no more
than acting as Englishmen were bound to act; his
proclamation of 'war to the death' was hastily issued and
early rescinded. It is not too much to say that if those
who from Madrid attempted to direct the relations
between Spain and her American possessions at this
crisis had been as truly Spanish as were the leaders of
revolt in the New World, the course of the struggle
would have been different, and that the Spanish empire
might still be in existence to-day. It was not on the
side of the revolutionary leaders, but on the side of the
home authorities that a non-Spanish outlook appears;
it was the home authorities and the commanders whom
they sent across the Atlantic who were really anti-
Spanish in temperament and in ideas. For, once more,
the War of Independence was an attempt to realize
the ideals of the race, to make possible the attainment
at one and the same time of liberty and efficient government.

VI

THE TRUE CHARACTER OF THE WAR
OF INDEPENDENCE

THE War of Independence was neither anti-Spanish nor non-Spanish. It was not the outcome of the spread of ideas recently imported from Europe or of some sudden awakening of political life, produced by the reception of eighteenth-century philosophic theories or by such events as the successful revolt of the English colonies in North America and the French Revolution. Its causes may none the less be found in the period which immediately preceded its occurrence. It may with some reason be contended that if the character of that period had been different, the dissolution of the political union between Spain and Spanish America would not have been effected or would at least have been very long postponed. For the War of Independence may be best described as a protest against the abandonment of the old, and Spanish, system of colonial administration and the attempt to substitute for it a new system, of which the spirit was not Spanish. Under the auspices of the Bourbon dynasty, and more especially under those of Charles III, changes were introduced which were distasteful to the creoles and the *mestizos*, since they offended at once the racial love of local and individual freedom and the racial love of efficient government.

That such changes should have been effected is no reflection upon the excellence of intention of those responsible for them. It is probable that no kings who sat upon the Spanish throne from the days of Ferdinand and Isabella onwards were more genuinely inspired by a desire to rule for the good of their subjects than were the first three monarchs of the Bourbon house. Philip V, perhaps, was too wayward and too much under the influence of his termagant wife, Elizabeth Farnese, to be an ideal ruler; in his later years he developed a species of melancholia which at least bordered upon insanity, and both his abdication and his resumption of his crown indicated an unbalanced mind. But Ferdinand VI, during his relatively brief reign, showed himself to be almost the model of an enlightened despot; he was one of the most amiable of all the long line of Spanish kings. Charles III shared the amiability of his half-brother and proved in Italy before his accession that he was possessed of no mean ability. On the Spanish throne he fulfilled the promise which he had shown on that of Naples, and he was well seconded by his ministers, Esquilache and Florida Blanca.

Yet in Spain itself, his government encountered more serious opposition than had been met by any government since the days of the *comuneros*, while in America it aroused discontent and resentment. The very achievement which Florida Blanca, in a letter to the king, described as the crowning glory of his administration, the definitive acquisition of Colonia, was a source of dissatisfaction in the province of Buenos Aires, a dissatisfaction which would have been greater had it not been modified by admiration for the capacity and brilliance of Ceballos, the first holder of the newly-created viceroyalty. The very acts, by which the home government sought to remove colonial grievances and to conform the administration to colonial wishes, were productive of exactly contrary results. The formal recognition of the colonies as being colonies was, perhaps, of small importance, although the change was rather unpopular than popular in Spanish America. The tendency which appeared to entrust the highest offices to men of inferior birth and lower rank than had been the viceroys and captains-general in the past, was rather unwise than wise, although here again no very strong feeling was aroused. It was far otherwise with those changes which were more clearly dictated by the 'enlightenment' and 'liberalism' of the sovereign. Administrative changes were brought about, economic reforms were carried through; the one and the other served not to conciliate, but to alienate the colonists. A ready ear was lent to the accusations brought against the Jesuits; they were expelled. It is significant enough that when deputies from the colonies attended the Cortes, after the later establishment of constitutional government in Spain, their first and most earnest request was that the Fathers should be restored to them.

The Bourbon kings, in fact, failed, as their relatives afterwards failed during the period of their exclusion from the French throne, to learn anything. The Habsburgs in Spain had become more Spanish than the Spaniards. Charles V himself, born and educated in Flanders, compelled during his whole reign to devote much of his time and attention to the affairs of Italy and Germany, occupying an international position and almost cosmopolitan of necessity, nevertheless identified himself with the nation of his mother. His reputed selection of the Spanish language as that 'que Dios habla', and his choice of Yuste as his place of retirement, are no more than illustrations of the degree to which he learned to appreciate a land to which he had come as an alien king. The Bourbons in Spain remained French. They were, indeed, more truly French than their cousins at Versailles. Louis XV was content with the cynical reflection that the existing régime would last his lifetime and was wholly irresponsive to the ideas which animated and attracted his subjects. Charles III was the very exponent of the theories of the eighteenth-century French thinkers, whose influence is clearly traceable in almost all his actions.

To the Spanish people such failure to adopt or even to understand their feelings was peculiarly ungrateful. For they have always cared more for such understanding than has, perhaps, any other nation. They prize it more

highly, and if they find this quality in a man, they can
forgive him almost any other deficiency with the very
forgiveness of love. To one who has this gift, they will
readily accord devotion, and if he be a ruler they will
feel towards him a loyalty which is proof against all the
evils resulting from tyranny or from incapacity; in such
a man they can pardon crimes and from such a man
they can endure grievous wrongs. They can and will do
even more. They will forget that the crimes have been
committed and that the wrongs have been inflicted.
But if a man have it not, it avails little that he has all
else. Admiration may perhaps be rendered to ability
and respect to virtue; gratitude may be felt for benefits
received. But the admiration is cold, the respect unwilling, the gratitude that which is felt towards one to
whom they are under a wholly unwelcome obligation.
With all their faults, the Habsburg kings acquired an
understanding of their people, and Philip II can assas-
sinate his son, his successors can watch negligently the
ruin of a once flourishing monarchy, without thereby
forfeiting the loyalty of their subjects. With all their
merits, the Bourbon kings lacked such an understanding, and Ferdinand VI can be almost a crowned saint,
Charles III a pattern of the enlightened ruler, without
thereby securing any hold upon the imagination of their
people. Liberals, of a later date, looking back upon the
reigns of these two sovereigns, have, indeed, borne testi-
mony to the excellence of the principles by which they
were inspired. The contemporaries of those same
sovereigns were far colder in their appreciation and were
inclined rather to lament the alien features of royal
policy than to applaud its enlightenment.

In the New World the character of the Bourbon
kings was disastrous for Spanish dominion. Under the
influence of French theories, they inaugurated a policy
which seemed to lack patriotic inspiration and which
involved a decided breach with a tradition which

had been maintained since the days of Columbus. Philip V opened the markets of his American possessions to French merchants, thereby securing to the inhabitants of those possessions at least a prospect of a somewhat readier supply of the commodities of which they stood in need. He might have been expected thereby to secure the approval of the colonists; on the contrary, he aroused in their minds a suspicion that he was prepared to sacrifice the interests of his kingdom to those of his native land. In the ensuing period, that economic policy which had been adopted by Ferdinand and Isabella and which had been followed by their successors, was first modified and then for all practical purposes abandoned. In place of the former annual fleets of merchant vessels, the sailings of which had, indeed, long been irregular, a service of register ships was theoretically established, and those ships were permitted to carry goods to the ports of Peru by way of Cape Horn. The original monopoly of Seville or Cadiz was destroyed by the formation of the Guipuzcoa Company and by the opening to oceanic trade of a number of ports upon both sides of the Atlantic. In the new Commercial Code, issued by Charles III, the various changes were confirmed and almost all the more hampering restraints upon colonial economic life were swept away. Intercourse between the various provinces in the New World was permitted; in place of the former highly protective system, an approach was made towards a policy of free trade. The court of Madrid was obviously influenced by the ideas of the 'Wealth of Nations' although that court forgot that Adam Smith himself had praised the Navigation Laws and had laid down that power is more important than prosperity.

The break with tradition was not confined to the economic sphere. In the course of the eighteenth century, the original administrative divisions were gradually abolished. Two new viceroyalties were

created, that of Nueva Granada, with its seat at Santa
Fé de Bogota, and that of La Plata, with its seat at
Buenos Aires. Chile, Guatemala, and Venezuela, as well
as Cuba, were erected into captaincies-general, and were
thereby practically exempted from the viceregal authority under which they nominally remained. The former
limits of the jurisdiction of the *audiencias* were corre-
spondingly modified, less, as has been the case in the
sixteenth and seventeenth centuries, in order to meet
the needs of expanding territorial dominion and of an
increasing population by the provision of new tribunals,
than in order to ensure a stricter supervision of the lower
courts. During the greater part of the colonial period,
the administration had been permeated by that deeply
religious spirit which characterized Spain in her golden
age and which was so essentially Spanish. In the
eighteenth century, the attitude of the government
changed. It did not, indeed, become secular, but it
appeared to be less carefully attentive to the interests
of religion. Not without some justice, the expulsion of
the Jesuits was attributed by their friends to the
influence gained by free-thinkers in the councils of
Charles III, and the control which the Church had
formerly exercised over education was impaired in the
interests of greater liberty of opinion.

The action of Ferdinand VI in employing Juan and
Ulloa to draw up a confidential report upon Spanish
America, which was dictated by a desire to discover
existing evils in order that they might be remedied, was
equally a breach of former practice. Every viceroy had,
indeed, drawn up an account of the area under his
jurisdiction, but these reports had been in their very
nature rather a defence than a criticism of the existing
order, any suggestions for change were suggestions for
change from within and by means of the ordinary action
of constituted authority. From the time of Las Casas
onwards attacks upon the system of government had

been formulated; at the close of the seventeenth century, that curious personality, Gabriel Fernández de Villalobos, had addressed his *Vaticinios de la Perdida de las Indias* to Charles II, and had depicted the condition of Spanish America as being so deplorable that only he himself was capable of devising and of effecting the remedies required. But these attacks had been written by men who were Spanish in temperament, a quality possessed even by Las Casas, and had also been unofficial; they had not been inspired by the home government and they had not been conceived in a non-Spanish spirit. Juan and Ulloa were certainly Spaniards, but they were not in harmony with their own race. Ulloa was a Fellow of the Royal Society and had fallen under English influences; both were products of the French spirit. The *Noticias Secretas* was inspired not by religious fervour, as had been the most denunciatory pamphlets of Las Casas, but by that eighteenth-century humanitarianism which had little regard for Christianity. The attack contained in it was also officially authorized, and was probably even commanded. It is very unlikely that it would have been what it was, had not its authors been assured in advance that the royal wish was that they should produce as scathing an indictment as possible of everything Spanish in Spanish America. The book amounted to a declaration that the whole colonial government was rotten to the core, that the Church was altogether corrupt, that the creoles were in the main inhuman, that a complete change in the methods and in the spirit of the administration was essential. In other words, it asserted that the tradition which had been followed hitherto was evil and that it should be abandoned.

To the Spanish Americans, the reversal of earlier policy by the Bourbon kings was the more unwelcome by reason of the very idealism of the race. In the political sphere, that idealism has always been con-

servative. It has looked more to that which has been
than to that which might be. It has aspired rather to
return to an old order, perhaps to an imaginary old
order, than to inaugurate a new. Of those English
reformers who have achieved success, the majority have
been almost scrupulous in asserting that they desired
no more than to sweep away abuses which had arisen
to corrupt a once well-nigh perfect state; they have
realized that openly to propose innovations would be
to alienate opinion in advance. The most successful
Spanish reformers have equally declared their conservatism, but with this difference, that they have not
only professed a longing to return to that which was,
but have also believed that such would be the effect of
the measures which they have advocated. It was to the
fact that she so fully shared in her people's reverence
for the past that Isabella the Catholic owed her extra-
ordinary success; it was that which very largely won
for her the devotion of Castile and which enabled her
to carry through reforms both in Church and state
which would have been bitterly opposed if they had
been professedly designed to introduce a new order.
So deeply rooted in the minds of the Spanish race is
this belief in the excellence of that which has been, that
it has survived even the satire of Cervantes; his genius
availed, perhaps, to shake the faith of his fellow-countrymen in their divinely ordained mission, but it did not
avail to convert them to a new faith, to lead them to
rest their hope on the future, save in so far as they trust
that the future may reproduce the past.

In the New World, no less than in Spain, the Bourbon kings thus outraged the sentiments of their subjects. The changes which they effected were professedly
changes; the reversal of the old order was openly
proclaimed. They displayed neither the reality nor
the pretence of respect for the past; they were as un-
appreciative of the value of tradition and of the merit of

continuity of development as were the most radical of
the French revolutionaries. In all that they did, in all
that they attempted to do, they by implication condemned their predecessors; by implication they held
up to reprobation the very rulers whom their subjects
so revered, Ferdinand and Isabella, Charles and Philip,
the creators of that administrative and economic system
which they were destroying. By sanctioning that indictment of the past, which is contained in the *Noticias
Secretas*, they placed themselves out of accord with
the views of those whose welfare they were sincerely
anxious to promote; they almost made a parade of their
non-Spanish outlook; they proved themselves to lack
understanding of their subjects.

If thereby they offended the idealism of the Spanish
Americans, they not less wounded their pride. In the
Noticias Secretas, it was not merely the administration
which was condemned; every member of the Spanish
population was almost equally singled out for castigation.
It is hard to estimate the effect of this upon a proud and
sensitive people. From one whom they could feel to be,
despite all, really one of themselves, even such rebukes
might have been tolerated; the diatribes of Las Casas did
not earn for him more than the aversion of those who
were most immediately affected and did not prevent him
from acquiring an undeserved reputation as an honest, if
misguided, critic. From Juan and Ulloa, and from the
monarchs who authorized their report, such an attack
upon all that they had revered and upon almost every
individual creole and *mestizo* was hardly to be borne;
it was the less to be borne when it was made the basis
of action by the government. Subconsciously, perhaps, but none the less deeply, it was felt that they had
fallen under alien rule and that they were required to
render obedience to a new order devised not by Spaniards but by thinly disguised Frenchmen or Englishmen.
From that moment, the idea of dissolving the political

union with Spain gained ground, not because Spanish
government was hated, but because it seemed that the
government had ceased to be Spanish in anything but
mere name. It was by no chance that the conspiracy
of Gramuset and Bernay in Chile, the first occasion upon
which the establishment of independence was definitely
contemplated, occurred at the very time when the
tenour of the report of Juan and Ulloa was becoming
generally known; the two facts are definitely and closely
related.

Outraging of sentiment and injury to pride would,
perhaps, have almost sufficed in themselves to have
produced in the minds of the Spanish Americans an
inclination to sever their connexion with the home
country. But that inclination was all the greater
because the new régime, established by the Bourbons,
also impaired the local and individual freedom of the
colonists, while it failed to produce efficient government. Under the rule of the Habsburgs, the colonists
have enjoyed practical liberty while enduring theoretical
restraint; under the Bourbons, they rather endured
practical restraints, while enjoying theoretical liberty.
A greater measure of freedom of trade was conceded to
them. It ceased to be illegal to import goods except
through Vera Cruz, Porto Bello or Cartagena, and
Buenos Aires; the merchants of Lima were no longer
able to fix the price of all commodities lawfully imported from Europe in the greater part of the viceroyalty of Peru. Some effort was made to encourage,
rather than to repress, colonial industries; colonial
productions were ensured a more widely extended
market and the more optimistic of the authorities in
Spanish America dreamed of a day when those productions should be freely used in England and when such
a change should be brought about that Bogota tea
would replace that of China in English households.

These apparent concessions, however, were very

largely unreal. Prior to the accession of the Bourbons
the economic regulations, issued for the colonies, had
been very generally a dead letter. A flourishing contraband trade had ensured a supply of many commodities
which might not be legally imported and if the prices
paid for them were somewhat exorbitant, so were the
prices of European goods in all non-European countries.
Under the new dynasty, a serious effort was made to
confine economic intercourse with the foreigner within
the limits prescribed by law, and this effort was not
entirely unsuccessful. A coastguard service was organized; authorities who had once connived at smuggling
ceased to do so, and while many regulations were
relaxed, those which were retained were more fully
enforced. The prices of contraband goods rose to still
greater heights; their supply was reduced. The supply
of non-contraband goods did not become adequate to
meet the demand; the price of those goods did not
fall. The greater liberty conceded was, in fact, less than
that which had been previously usurped; the concessions
made to colonial interests were to a great extent nullified by a simultaneous limitation of illegal freedom.

At the same time financial policy became more
stringent. The Habsburg kings had imposed a number
of dues upon the inhabitants of Spanish America, but
they had been somewhat easy tax-gatherers, since they
had relied mainly on the output of the mines and on
the valuable natural products of the New World as
sources of revenue. Their financial regulations were
no more strictly enforced than were their commercial;
any hardship involved was rather theoretical than
actual. The vigorous opposition of the colonists to
the introduction of the *alcabala*, the tax upon sales,
was an expression of hatred for a particular imposition
and not of revolt against financial oppression. With the
accession of the Bourbons, however, the situation was
altered. The very effort which was made to lighten

the burden of taxation and to render its incidence more equitable necessitated a stricter insistence upon the payment of such dues as were still payable. The very benevolence of the government involved an increased expenditure; public works were undertaken which were of undoubted utility but the execution of which proved to be also very costly. The attempt to revive the naval and military power of Spain imposed a further tax upon colonial resources. Demands for increased revenue were continually addressed to the authorities in the New World and even the partial satisfaction of these demands led to considerable discontent, which developed at times into open resistance. The measures of Gonzalez Blanco produced a riot at Santiago de Chile; the financial policy of Gutierrez de Piñéres in Nueva Granada was the cause of the rising of the *comuneros*. Both the commercial and the financial policy of the Bourbons, in fact, enforced restrictions which in the past had existed, but had been largely evaded; the colonists enjoyed less individual freedom under the enlightened monarchs of the eighteenth century than they had enjoyed in the sixteenth and seventeenth centuries under kings who had hardly laid claim to be either philanthropists or philosophers.

Local liberty, a possession prized no less highly than individual liberty, was similarly restricted by the administrative changes which were effected. During the Habsburg period, there had been a very considerable divergence between the theory and the fact of Spanish government in the New World. The two viceroys were far away from the greater part of the territories which they nominally ruled; the authorities more immediately on the spot, while free from control from Mexico or Lima, were yet not invested with sufficient power to be able to dominate their districts with any completeness. The *cabildo* was free from the *audiencia*, the *audiencia* was independent of the governor, the governor could constantly escape the control of the viceroy; local autonomy was the rule, subordination to the central government the exception. To reverse this order was the purpose of the reforms carried out during the eighteenth century, and while the purpose was not really attained, a sufficient approach to attainment was made to limit the freedom which had previously existed. The central authority was brought nearer to the various districts, the more so because the captains-general enjoyed approximately viceregal powers. The new administrative system did not ostensibly produce revolt, but it none the less increased the restlessness of the colonial population, dissatisfied with the breach of tradition, impatient of heavier financial burdens, and offended by the limitation of a once almost complete individual freedom.

It is perhaps possible that the resentment caused by well-intentioned measures, the spirit of which was yet alien from the Spanish temper, would have been lessened if the changes introduced had resulted in that efficient government which they were very largely designed to secure. Such efficiency, however, was no more attained under the Bourbons than it had been under the Habsburgs. The attempt to establish more direct and more complete control rendered the task of administration more laborious and more complex. It was at the same time rendered more difficult. The influence of the Jesuits had been consistently exerted in favour of the existing régime down to the reign of Charles III; the value of that influence was demonstrated at Quito, only two years before the order for expulsion was issued, the Fathers quelling a riot in that city with which the civil authorities had been unable to cope. The overthrow of the Society deprived the Spanish government in America of a powerful ally. The step was the more disastrous because it was a serious break with tradition and because it led to neglect of education

and to the falling of such education as endured into
the hands of men who were not well disposed towards
the existing order.

That increased control which was desired was not
in actual fact secured. The regulations of the Bourbons
were more irksome than those of the Habsburgs because
they were followed by somewhat spasmodic attempts
at enforcement, which irritated opinion and yet failed
to produce the intended result. Despite the destruction
of Colonia as a basis of contraband trade, that trade
continued in the La Plata district; despite the organization of a more elaborate coastguard service, smuggling
was general on the shores of the Caribbean Sea. The
establishment of a larger defence force failed to protect
the coast towns against foreign attack and thus served
rather to emphasize the impotence of the authorities.
The fact that the most serious native revolt, that led
by Tupac Amaru, the descendant and namesake of
the Inca executed in the sixteenth century, followed
the expulsion of the Jesuits and the development of the
changed system of administration, is significant. The
prevalent restlessness produced among the creoles and
mestizos, emboldened the Indians to make an attempt
which at an earlier date they would have felt to be foredoomed to failure and which they would perhaps have
felt no desire to undertake. The Bourbons had, indeed,
undermined the foundations of Spanish power and
hurried on the decline and fall of their empire in the
New World by the very measures which were intended
to consolidate that power and to preserve that empire.

It is true that inefficiency of government was no new
thing in Spanish America, but that inefficiency was far
more serious under the Bourbons than it had been
under the Habsburgs. Down to the eighteenth century
the creoles had been able to entertain the illusion that
their rulers ruled, even when those rulers were in fact
most impotent. That illusion was aided by the preva-

lent uncertainty as to the exact powers of any particular
branch of the administration, by the fact that a local
authority might be overruled by the sudden intervention of the distant viceroys at Lima or Mexico, and by
the not entirely unwarranted supposition that royal
commands, which were not obeyed, were not in fact
expressions of the true will of the king. The administrative reforms of the Bourbons rendered the enter-
tainment of this illusion far more difficult. It was not
merely that by the subdivision of the viceroyalties and
by the creation of captaincies-general, the central
government was brought into far closer contact with
the various districts, with the result that resistance to
that government appeared far more clearly as that
which in truth it was. The very virtues of the Bourbon
kings endangered the preservation of their dominions.
During the whole period from the death of Philip II
to that of Charles II royal policy had been wavering
and uncertain; measures had been adopted and abandoned, orders issued and revoked, as the favourites who
controlled the kings rose and fell. In such circumstances,
those who wished to believe that the crown was never
resisted and that the monarch ruled effectively were
supplied with a plausible explanation of anything which
might suggest that such belief was unfounded. Under
the more virile sovereigns of the Bourbon line, and more
especially under Charles III, royal policy was firm and
consistent, contradictions disappeared, carelessness was
replaced by vigour, favourites by ministers. It is very
significant to compare the reception given in Spanish
America to the order for the expulsion of the Jesuits
with that which had been given some two hundred years
before to the order for the enforcement of the 'New
Laws'. In the earlier case, active and passive opposition
had been offered to an unpopular decree, and those who
resisted had declared that the enactments misrepresented the will of Charles V. The decree against the

Jesuits, although less obviously detrimental to the
material welfare of the colonists, was equally unpopular
in many districts. It was not the less obeyed, even by
such officials as Guill y Gonzaga, governor of Chile,
who was devoted to the Society, and even in such
places as Santa Fé and Quito, where popular feeling
was almost dangerously on the side of the Fathers. It
was no longer possible to contend that disobedience
was obedience; it needed a great exercise of faith, if
faith could be the capacity for believing that which is
known to be untrue, to be convinced that a royal order
was not intended to be carried out. There could no
longer be any uncertainty concerning the actual will
of the king.

In such circumstances it became clear that resistance
was nothing but resistance, that orders which were
not enforced were yet indeed royal orders, that inefficiency was indeed inefficiency, that the government
did indeed fail to govern effectively. The administration
obviously failed to satisfy either of the two dominating
aspirations of the race. While local and individual
freedom was impaired efficiency was not secured. As
these facts became more and more generally appreciated,
resentment deepened and spread. It was increased by
a more acute recognition of grievances which had once
been almost tolerated as if they were inevitable. The
creoles became less ready to submit to their continued
normal exclusion from high office, especially when the
capacity of some among them for such office was recognized by appointment to it; the *mestizos* became less
ready to accept perpetual subordination; the very
Indians were moved towards a new self-assertion. That
of good which there was in the Spanish administration
was more and more forgotten or denied; that which
there was of evil was more and more recognized and
even exaggerated. Sentiments which might have been no
more than vaguely felt were expressed in telling phrases

borrowed from France and justified upon abstract principles which rendered them more attractive to an idealistic race. A wider circulation of literature among a people, no longer educated to accept the existing order, secured a wider acceptance of doctrines tending towards a subversion of that order.

It may still be questioned whether dissatisfaction would have sufficed to produce a desire for independence, save in a few minds, had it not been that such a desire was fostered by the special circumstances of the moment. The Spanish race is temperamentally loyal, and loyal to the monarchical idea. It is a noteworthy fact that, after the Middle Ages, no Spanish sovereign was ever deposed or assassinated, until Isabella II was driven to abdicate, and that in her case there was some doubt concerning her title to the throne. It was not that the monarchs merited devotion; on the contrary, Philip III was incompetent, Philip IV was an inferior copy of his father, Charles II was a half-human imbecile, Charles IV was a weakling dominated by the reputed paramour of his wife. It was that their subjects rendered to them a loyalty which they did not deserve; that for the occupant of the throne, whatever manner of man he might be, they felt an almost religious veneration. As long as that occupant was to be clearly identified, as long as the legitimate object of loyalty was certain, no movement towards independence was likely to be attended with any great success. An attempt in Chile which was, significantly enough, organized by two Frenchmen and not by Spaniards at all, was half concealed and was wholly unsuccessful. The expedition of Miranda occupied Coro on the Venezuelan coast; the people of the district were very far from being thereby roused to aid in the winning of independence.

The attempt of Napoleon to place his brother on the Spanish throne produced a changed situation. Various claimants to the loyalty of the colonists appeared; for the first time in the history of the Spanish empire in the New World the identity of the lawful sovereign was uncertain. At the same time, they felt some reluctance to accept any of the claims put forward. Charles IV and his son were prisoners in France; Joseph Bonaparte was an alien; the Supreme Junta, claiming to act for Ferdinand VII, was a revolutionary body, unknown to Spanish tradition and possessed only of the most dubious legitimacy. Spain, in fact, seemed to have fallen completely under the control of foreign or of non-Spanish influences, and those who would have perhaps been otherwise content to wait for the changes which they desired until the day when a true Spanish king should once more occupy the throne, were moved to feel that such waiting would be in vain. A conviction gained ground and was confirmed by the defeat of the British attempt on Buenos Aires, that nothing could be achieved save by the efforts of the colonists themselves, and that it was necessary to dissolve the union with Spain, if Spanish America were to remain Spanish.

From this the War of Independence was born. The conviction was never universal among the colonists. Creoles and *mestizos* figured in both the contending parties, and so figured from a sincere belief in the cause which they supported. Nothing, indeed, could be further from the truth than to suppose that the struggle was waged by Spanish Americans against the 'Europeans'; it was a struggle of Spanish Americans against Spanish Americans. Neither party was in any real sense anti-Spanish, although the one desired to dissolve and the other to maintain political union with Spain. Nor were the principles of either party non-Spanish. Nothing was further from the thoughts of the champions of independence than any idea of creating some new order which should be French or English in character; they desired neither the subordination of the individual to the state which was achieved by the French Revolu-

tion as interpreted by Napoleon, or that subordination
of the state to the individual which was characteristic
of England. They desired, as their opponents desired,
to achieve the realization of the twin Spanish aspirations which had been so palpably not satisfied under the
Bourbon dynasty.

The difference between the two parties in the war
was thus not one of aim but of method. Both desired
to reach the same goal, but whereas some believed that
it could be reached only by the avenue of independence,
others believed that it could be reached without the
dissolution of the union with Spain. It is to this fact
that the bitterness of the conflict in many districts may
be most justly attributed. It is always far easier to
understand a radical divergence of ideals than to
appreciate a reluctance to adopt a particular method of
attaining an ideal. Neither party in the war was quite
able to see why the members of the opposing party were
in opposition. The conflict was essentially internecine
and was therefore marked by all that intolerance which
is invariably found in the strife of brothers. To the
same cause may be attributed the fluctuations of
fortune, the fact that the issue appeared to be so long
in doubt that there have not been wanting some to
suggest that the ultimate triumph of the cause of
independence was due rather to the action of Canning
and Monroe than to the efforts of the Spanish Americans
themselves. It was long before the majority of the
colonists were convinced that to break with Spain was
essential.

They would perhaps have never been so convinced
and the break would perhaps never have become essential, had Ferdinand VII and his advisers understood
and shared in the temper of the Spanish race. In
the sixteenth century, Gonzalo Pizarro had led a
revolt in Peru, and if he lacked the daring to proclaim himself an independent sovereign, the thought

was in the minds of some of his followers, such as the
notorious 'Demonio de los Andes', and its realization
was within the bounds of possibility. That the revolt
was quelled and that Peru was so easily restored to the
full obedience of Charles V is not to be attributed
primarily to the conviction of the rebels that if they
did not speedily submit, they would be forced to do
so by an expedition from Spain. It was due rather
to the method which was adopted to meet a critical
situation. The Council of the Indies realized the true
nature of that situation; they understood that those
who were in rebellion were not at heart disloyal to
Spain or to their king, and that if it would be an easy
matter to drive them into disloyalty, it would also be
an easy matter to win them back to their allegiance.
The Spaniard is proud and by temper independent;
he can with difficulty be compelled, but he can be
persuaded and led. It was by leadership, not by compulsion, that Ferdinand and Isabella effected the re-
generation of their country; by persuasion, not by force.
It was by the same methods that the advisers of their
grandson ended the revolt of Gonzalo Pizarro. They
sent to the New World no army, no general, but Pedro
de la Gasca, a simple ecclesiastic, who possessed the
essential quality of understanding.

Had Ferdinand VII sent to America, not would-be
brilliant military expeditions, not supposedly skilled
commanders, but some shabbily dressed ecclesiastic,
coming without pomp and display, but equipped with
an understanding of his fellow-countrymen, it is more
than probable that the whole history of Spanish America
would have been changed. The very leaders of the
revolution were themselves notably reluctant to throw
off their allegiance; the declarations of independence
read almost as so many gestures of despair, not as so many
expressions of joyous hope. It needed little enough to
rally the majority of the colonists once more round the

throne, for that majority was at once conservative and royalist. It needed little enough, but it needed that little most emphatically. Ferdinand VII did not understand. He had imbibed political ideas which were not Spanish, and his conduct towards the Spanish Americans was such as could only serve to arouse undying hostility. He attempted to drive where he should have endeavoured to lead, to compel where he should have persuaded, and he paid the penalty of his ignorance of the mentality of those with whom he had to deal. He created in the New World an overwhelming body of opinion in favour of the view that only by dissolution of their union with Spain could the colonists hope to realize those ideals which, as Spaniards by culture and tradition, they so highly prized. Charles III, by his attempt to establish a system of administration which was un-Spanish, was responsible for the beginning of the movement which culminated in independence. Ferdinand VII, by his adoption of an un-Spanish method of dealing with the crisis which had arisen, was most truly responsible for the victory of the colonists. Spanish America ceased to be part of the empire of Spain because the Bourbon kings failed to understand the circumstances which had enabled that empire to endure, because they were not Spaniards by temperament, because it was only by becoming independent that the colonies could retain that character which had been impressed upon them by the conquerors of the New World.

VII

THE ESTABLISHMENT OF REPUBLICS

BOTH the leaders of the movement which culminated in the establishment of the Spanish American republics, and the overwhelming majority of their followers, were Spaniards or were men imbued with Spanish ideas. They were idealists who were yet convinced that if an ideal is to be attainable, it must not be wholly divorced from the material; they pursued not abstractions but concrete realities; they were essentially practical men seeking to reach essentially practical results. By temper they were far more truly conservative than radical; they were rather reformers than revolutionaries; they were believers in continuity of development and were by no means eager to break with the past.

Towards Spain they felt not hatred but love. Their hostility was directed not against the mother country, but against those who ruled at Madrid, and their professions of loyalty to the crown, so far from being merely idle words, were the expression of heartfelt conviction. It is true that, at an early date in the history of the movement, the feeling gradually gained ground, until it was generally entertained, that dissolution of the political union with Spain was a necessity, but it is also true that it was regarded as a regrettable necessity. The desire for independence was not one for independence for its own sake, as an end in itself, but for independence as a means to an end. That end was the realization of the ideals of the race, neither of which had been realized by the régime established by the Bourbon kings, and to realization of which Ferdinand VII appeared to be irrevocably opposed.

The movement was accordingly not of necessity a republican movement, nor was it at all certain at first that it would eventually result in the creation of

republican states. On the contrary, that it should so
develop was not the wish of the most eminent leaders
in the war. Bolivar set before himself the ideal of a
wide dictatorship which should embrace the greater
part, if not the whole, of Spanish America; of a veiled
monarchy, the natural evolution of which would have
been in the direction of an autocracy rather than of a
democracy. Belgrano dreamed of a vast empire, of
a revival and an extension of the old dominion of the
Incas, remodelled upon Spanish principles. San Martin
favoured some analogue of that system actually created
in Brazil when the heir of Portugal decided to prefer
his colonial to his hereditary realm.

Among the leaders, in fact, monarchists were rather
the rule than the exception, and there is no reason to
believe that they were out of sympathy with the
majority of their followers. It is significant that the
failure of Bolivar's scheme for a great republic which
should include the modern states of Venezuela,
Colombia, Ecuador, Peru, and Bolivia, was due rather
to the fact that he was unable to exercise direct personal
authority over so wide an area than to any opposition
to the exercise of such an authority in any part of that
area. Each district objected not to his presence, but to
his absence; Colombia declared that it could no longer
recognize him when he was resident in Peru, but it
received him with acclamation and endowed him once
more with the fullest powers when he returned to
Bogotá.

Nor, despite a popular impression and explicit assertions, was the movement essentially inspired by democratic ideas, save in so far as the conception of individual
liberty is one purely democratic. The leaders were by
temperament aristocratic; they were believers in social
divisions while they were not less believers in equality
of treatment for all classes. They were in fact Spaniards,
and had their ideas been carried into effect, the new

states would have been organized rather upon the model of Spain, so far as social conditions were concerned, than upon the model of the United States. Those distinctions, which were explicitly abolished in the constitutions, would either not have been abolished or would have been in due course revived. It is hard to see how any other result could have followed had the empire of Belgrano's dreams been created, or had the kingdoms desired by others been formed; it is by no means improbable that the same result would have ensued if the schemes of Bolivar had been realized. The actual abolition of titles of honour was due rather to the fact that there was no one to confer such titles upon those who had most merited them, the generals in the war, than to any intrinsic objection to nobility. There is, indeed, no evidence of any rooted dislike for those class distinctions which had been recognized in colonial times.

Least of all, perhaps, was the movement intended to bring about the establishment of representative institutions in the English or North American sense. At the beginning of the struggle juntas were called into existence in most cities; as the struggle developed national assemblies were convoked. But neither the one nor the other derived its inspiration from any land save Spain; the assemblies might borrow their names from France or the United States, and their ostensible form, but they borrowed nothing else. Both they and the juntas were emphatically Spanish in origin. They were a revival of the *cabildo abierto*, the general gathering of all the citizens, which had been once a feature of the municipal life of every city and town in Castile. Any representative character which was assumed by these bodies was the result of necessity and not of imitation of foreign models. As the cities and towns which were privileged to form the Cortes had sent their proctors, so districts sent their proctors to the national assemblies of the Spanish American embryo states. The reason for the sending was the same in both cases, the physical impossibility of the attendance of all the inhabitants. Some significance attaches to the fact that in the smaller states, the Central American republics, a unicameral system has been adopted, and that a bicameral system has been established elsewhere only after some apparent hesitation. The idea of a single chamber was more in accord with Spanish American ideas than that of a congress of two chambers, and the ultimate acceptance of the latter idea was perhaps due to the difficulty of constituting in the larger states any one body which should even distantly approximate to an assembly of the whole people, to the *cabildo abierto*.

If the decision taken in favour of a republican, democratic, and representative organization were not due to any decided preference for such a form of organization, it was still less due to admiration for English, French or North American institutions. The absence of any such admiration is noticeable in the political proposals of the leaders in the War of Independence. The constitution which Bolivar drew up for the republic which had adopted his name is rather more reminiscent of Athens or Rome than of London or Paris. The underlying spirit of the letter, which he addressed at the same time to the people of Bolivia, was conceived in a Castilian spirit; the sentiments expressed in it can be found in the addresses presented to Enrique IV, the immediate predecessor of Isabella the Catholic. There is little enough evidence that the adoption of a republican form of government was the outcome of free and unfettered choice.

It can, indeed, hardly be doubted that a single monarchy or a number of monarchies, and not a number of republics, would have been established, had it not been found at a very early date that to do so was impossible. Even if the union of all Spanish America, or of all Spanish South America, in a single state had not been a somewhat idle dream, realization of which was rendered impossible by mere extent of territory, difficulty of communication, divergence of interest and local antipathies, there would still have been no suitable candidate for the projected throne. The only possible sovereign would have been Ferdinand VII, who would have been wholly unwilling to transfer his residence from the Old World to the New, and who was in reality quite unfitted for such a position. The idea of a number of kingdoms was no more feasible in fact, although much more feasible in theory, since there was a dearth of suitable candidates for the thrones of such realms. No Spanish princes were available, and had they been available they would hardly have been willing to place themselves in opposition to the recognized head of their house. To a non-Spanish prince, there appeared to be fundamental objections. If the Bourbons, reigning in Spain for a century, had yet failed to appreciate the feelings of their subjects, it was hardly likely that members of some other royal house would do so. It was far more likely that the Spanish Americans would find that they had placed themselves under the rule of men even less acceptable than the monarch whose control they had been forced to reject. Nor in any case was it at all probable that any European prince would have been prepared to cross the Atlantic in order to accept a revolutionary crown in an age when revolution was the accursed thing in all the monarchical circles of the Old World, and in lands which were then little known and which were perhaps regarded as being hardly more civilized than Bornu or the country of the Hottentots.

It was such a lack of possible candidates in Europe that perhaps suggested to some of the monarchically-minded leaders that kings might be found in America itself. Belgrano, like Miranda before him, momentarily

entertained the somewhat fantastic idea of creating
a South American empire under a descendant of the
Incas of Peru. There was some disposition to idealize
the native of pre-conquest days; the thought of re-
dressing some imaginary wrong and of restoring the
Indians to the position of which they were supposed
to have been deprived, made some appeal to the enthusiasm of an enthusiastic moment. Little reflection, however, was needed to secure conviction of the imprac-
ticability of any such solution of the problem. The
pride of the Spaniards would not have permitted their
subordination to the rule of any sovereign drawn from
a race which had been for centuries under their control,
and which they regarded as being morally and mentally
inferior. There would have been even more obvious
objection to the accession of some native than to that
of a non-Spanish European prince. It would further
have probably proved to be impossible to discover the
legitimate heir to the crown of Atahualpa or Huascar;
the appearance of a number of rival claimants would
probably have resulted in civil war between their
various partisans.

From the other sections of the colonial population,
it was equally impossible to select men able to fill a
royal position. There were no creoles, so marked out
by descent, as to have any superiority of birth over all
their fellows; the exaltation of an equal to the throne
would infallibly have been fraught with the same consequences as was the usurpation of Iturbide in Mexico.
His short and troubled reign, the story of his extrava-
gance and ostentation, illustrate how impossible it was
that any Spanish American should become a monarch
in Spanish America.

The fact that no suitable candidates for thrones
were discoverable, coupled with the fact that to very
many personal government was to be preferred to any
other form of rules, suggested a compromise between

pure royalism and pure republicanism. To confer upon
one of themselves the royal title and an hereditary
position was generally felt to be so impossible as to
be beyond the range of practical politics. But to grant
to a man of eminence supreme power for life was
a more rational proposal. The establishment of such
a dictatorship was the ideal of Bolivar, who aspired to
the authority, although not to the name, of king, and
the arguments upon which he based his assertion that
only by such a system could stable and efficient government be secured were in themselves plausible and have,
in some measure, been vindicated by the subsequent
history of the republics. The Spanish Americans had
always been used to monarchical rule; they were unac-
customed to the idea of self-government save in local
affairs, and it could be reasonably suggested that they
lacked the experience necessary for the smooth working
of representative institutions even if such institutions
had been in accord with the temper of the race. The
political life to which they were accustomed, and for
which they might be accordingly supposed to be best
fitted, was political life under the direction of some
individual, and a dictatorship might thus seem to be
the method of government best suited to the conditions
which prevailed.

To the formal establishment of such a system, however, there were serious objections. If Bolivar himself
might seem to be well fitted to occupy so predominant
a position, if to such a position he might seem to be
entitled by the services which he had rendered, his case
was almost exceptional. It was difficult to suggest any
other names for a like position; among the various
other leaders, none, with the possible exceptions of San
Martin and Sucre, were sufficiently pre-eminent. At
the same time, the vigour of local feeling practically
precluded the effecting of such union between the
various districts that no more than one or two dictators

should be required. Each individual province felt that
in such an event it would probably see its interests
sacrificed to those of some other province and more
especially to those of that area in which the dictator
might fix his residence, and with which he would thus
become more closely identified. The difficulty, inherent in any such system, of finding a successor to the
supreme position on the death or retirement of any
actual occupant would, moreover, have been intensified
in Spanish America, where the choice could hardly have
been limited to any one section of the population. The
inevitable temptation to convert a life into an hereditary
office, or to endeavour to transmit power to some
personal favourite, would have been there far stronger;
numerous candidates would infallibly have appeared,
and decision between their rival claims would have
been in many cases impossible save by recourse to arms.
There was hardly less danger that a dictator would use
his authority to the prejudice of individual freedom,
the more so since the conception of an accountable
dictator was almost a contradiction in terms. Hence,
while the desire for efficient government impelled the
Spanish Americans to see political salvation in personal
rule, the impossibility of establishing a workable system,
combined with their practical idealism, urged them not
to concentrate power in the hands of any single man.
The fate which overtook those who in the first days of
independence achieved the supreme position reveals the
growth of the conviction that the creation of explicitly
irresponsible dictatorships would be the creation of a
system likely to produce all the evils, and to secure few,
if any, of the advantages of hereditary monarchy.
Bolivar, the greatest of all the leaders, died in sorrow
and disillusionment, disappointed of his hopes. Sucre,
the foremost military genius of the war, perished by
assassination.

The decision was thus eventually taken to adopt a

republican government. Whatever might be the actual
organization of executive power, it was resolved to lay
down as a fundamental principle that sovereignty rested
with the people as a whole, and that it might be by them
resumed at any moment, while to them every holder
of authority was definitely responsible. It followed that
no permanent dictatorship could be legally created; it
was within the competence of the citizens temporarily
to grant dictatorial powers to the head of the executive,
but it was equally within their competence at any
moment to revoke these powers. The idealism of the
Spanish Americans impelled them to go somewhat
farther, and to insist emphatically upon the wholly
democratic character of the new states. It is somewhat
instructive to compare the constitutions which they
formed with that of the United States. The framers of
the latter document did not feel it to be necessary to do
more than to declare that 'to secure the blessings of
liberty' was among the objects of the constitution and
to forbid the creation of titles of honour or their
acceptance by citizens of the republic. The ten
original amendments to the constitution go no farther
than to proclaim the inviolability of the liberty of the
subject, to provide for the due administration of justice,
and to guard against the dangers of a standing army.
There is no declaration of the rights of man and of the
citizen; there is no insistence upon the democratic
character of the institutions established. On the other
hand, in the majority of the Spanish American constitutions there is such insistence. In them the fundamental
rights of the citizens are enumerated and explicitly
guaranteed, until it seems as if the authors of these
documents distrusted themselves and were anxious to
guard against their own distaste for the system which
they were engaged in erecting. The divergence so
revealed is only that which might be expected. The
North Americans of the days of Washington were

republicans by conviction and choice; the Spanish Americans of the days of Bolivar were republicans by compulsion. The former joyously embraced an opportunity which offered; the latter bowed somewhat sadly to necessity.

Republicanism, indeed, had never made any strong appeal to the Spanish race, whether in the Old World or in the New. It is significant of the attitude of the former colonists that the immediate cause of the declaration of Mexican independence was the occurrence in Spain of a revolution which deprived the king of absolute power, and that the 'Plan of Iguala' designed the creation of a kingdom under Ferdinand VII or of some prince of his house. One of the charges brought against Augustin Iturbide was that he had failed to carry out this plan, and that he had instead himself seized the crown. The decision in favour of a republican system of government was, indeed, very far from being the result of any deep conviction of the excellence of such a system. When it had been taken, no more had been accomplished than the partial solution of one of the problems by which the leaders of the War of Independence were confronted. That solution was essentially tentative. It was altogether uncertain whether the republics would be republics in fact, as well as in name, or whether they would be veiled monarchies; whether they would be indeed democratically governed states or despotisms slightly tempered by recognition of a constitutional right of revolt.

The step which had been taken was, moreover, emphatically no more than a preliminary step. Other and more difficult and more important problems remained to be settled. It had yet to be decided whether the republics should be unitary or federal, whether they should be mutually independent or in some manner linked together politically. Their area had equally to be defined. It was not yet clear whether wholly new lines of division should be drawn or whether those lines of division which had existed in the colonial period should be maintained. If the latter the unit of independence was still uncertain. If it had been decided that the unit should not be the two original viceroyalties, it had still to be decided whether it should be the later viceroyalties, or the captaincies-general, or the provincial governorships, or the areas controlled by the various *audiencias*. Everything, indeed, was still in a state of uncertainty, which was hardly removed by the formal promulgation of constitutions, since when those documents had been written and with all solemnity proclaimed, it had yet to be decided whether they would be genuinely accepted and whether they were in practice workable.

Upon all these points, no attempt was made to reach a decision upon theoretical grounds or in accordance with any abstract principles, nor, despite frequent assertions to the contrary, did the example of the United States exert any great influence, if it exerted any influence at all. The fact that in the event the Argentine, Mexico, and Venezuela became federal republics was the result of local circumstances; it was no tribute of admiration to the North Americans. The fact that the other states in the event became unitary republics was no indication of peculiar antipathy to the United States; it was equally the result of local circumstances. The Spanish Americans, indeed, approached the problems of state organization, not in a North American or in an English or in a French spirit, but in a Spanish spirit. The test which they applied to any proposed solution was not whether it conformed to some philosophical theory or whether it would be approved by some school of political thinkers or whether it had proved to be a satisfactory solution in some alien land. They sought only to discover whether, by its adoption, they would attain the realization, realization in the

Spanish sense, of their ideals. The history of the organization and of the development of the republics, their political life, is the history of continuous striving after a solution which should secure simultaneously local and personal liberty and efficiency of government, as the Spaniards understand liberty and efficiency.

VIII

FREEDOM IN SPANISH AMERICA

THE problem of securing at one and the same time the maximum of liberty, local and individual, and the maximum of efficiency in government, is one which has appeared in the history of every state which has possessed any conscious political life. The effort to find a solution for this problem has been a feature of the constitutional history of England. Under the Lancastrians, apparent liberty was secured at the price of certain inefficiency; under the Tudors, certain efficiency at the price of apparent servitude, while as a result of the Great Rebellion and of the Revolution, both ends were at least seemingly attained. In France, during the last period of the *ancien régime*, there was neither liberty nor efficiency; the French Revolution may be regarded as an attempt to secure both, an attempt of which the success was at least questionable. Imperial Germany supplied a very model of efficient government; the coincident restraint of liberty was perhaps one of the principal causes of the entire collapse of the imperial system under the stress of military defeat. In every land which can justly be regarded as civilized the problem has appeared and has been met with varying success.

But in no country has it assumed so acute a character or been so enduring as in Spain and her daughter states. The Spanish race has always been inspired by an intensity of love for local and personal liberty beyond that of any other race; it has always been proudly individualist. It has also been always deeply convinced of the value of efficient government. At the same time, it has always been idealist, with the result that the maximum of liberty desired has been the ideal maximum, the maximum of efficiency the ideal maximum. Other races have been content to accept solutions which

have admittedly fallen short of perfection; they have
effected some working compromise, and it is, perhaps,
because they have been willing to do so, that the
problem has for them very largely ceased to exist.
The English, more especially, have continually found
such illogical means of escape from a logical dilemma.
They have never been greatly concerned that the
ostensible and the actual form of their institutions
should be hopelessly at variance, and they have been
ready to find salvation in 'conventions of the constitution', to be unquestioning so long as in the main the
results have appeared to be satisfactory. The Spaniard,
however, has never been so content. Compromise to
him has always tended to be peculiarly abhorrent in
almost every relation of life, to appear as a somewhat
cowardly attempt to escape from the battle. He has
always been more ready to bear with the avowed pagan
than with the questionably orthodox, with the agnostic
than with the Protestant; much more hatred was felt
for the *conversos*, suspected Judaisers, than for the
professed Jews or the Moors. Unwillingness to compromise cost countless lives in the long wars in Morocco,
as it had cost countless lives in the Low Countries and
in many other parts of Europe. The solution of the
political problem is thus for him hardly to be attained;
even if some approach be made to the ideal a still
nearer approach is desired. Both in Spain and in Spanish
America, the search for perfection has always been
ardently prosecuted; in both lands, there has been the
same determination that perfection shall be indeed
perfection.

As the ultimate problem has thus remained insoluble,
so in the former colonies of Spain, those subordinate
problems which constitute its parts have attained
at most only a partial solution. In the republics,
neither the desire for local freedom nor the desire
for individual freedom nor the desire for efficiency

of government has perhaps ever been really satisfied; although in one or other of these states proximate satisfaction of one or other of these desires has been reached, that satisfaction has been no more than proximate, and has further been attained only by the postponement of any attempt to secure a like gratification of one or other of the three wishes. Efficiency has thus been in a measure secured at the cost of liberty, liberty at the cost of efficiency; satisfaction has never been complete or enduring or the search abandoned. A certain atmosphere of instability has thus been created, a certain restlessness which has sometimes been interpreted in Europe to mean that the race is by nature anarchical, prone to revolution, incapable of ordered political life. The Spanish Americans have, in fact, paid and continue to pay the penalty of their idealism, an idealism too sincere and too deep to be readily appreciated by other and more materialistic peoples.

Of the three desires, that for local liberty has been, perhaps, most nearly realized. In the Spanish race, local feeling has always been very intense; Spain herself has never been unified in the truest sense. As against the rest of Europe the Spaniards are indeed one people, as Europeans feel themselves to be one against Asiatics, but even to-day the Gallego is a foreigner in Andalusia, the Andalusian in Castile, the Castilian in Catalonia. In America, during the colonial period, local sentiment had been equally strong, and had been at once fostered and gratified by the almost necessary concession of a wide measure of autonomy to the various constituent parts of a vast empire. When independence was proclaimed it was no more than natural in the circumstances that such autonomy should be preserved and perhaps extended; it might seem that it was also natural that previously self-governing districts should be immediately erected into wholly independent states.

Such has been, in the main, the ultimate result of

the substitution of the republics for the Spanish empire, but the result was reached only with difficulty and by degrees. It was not the unanimous wish of the leaders in the War of Independence to perpetuate existing divisions; to some of them the common struggle in which all were engaged seemed to afford an admirable occasion for the obliteration of minor differences, in order that victory might lead to the establishment of a powerful state, of which the future should be no less glorious than had been the past of the mother country. The conflict between such champions of a fuller unity and those who were wedded to the cause of localism appeared even while the issue of the war was still in doubt. It produced a certain unwillingness to co-operate which was of no little advantage to the generals of Ferdinand VII. Even districts which were seriously menaced by the royalist commanders were somewhat reluctant to owe their deliverance to any efforts but their own. San Martin, advancing across the Andes to aid in the liberation of the Pacific lands, Bolivar and Sucre, advancing from the north for the same purpose, alike experienced the effect of localism. The enthusiasm with which the liberator was acclaimed in Bolivia was cooled as soon as a prospect appeared of some limitation of the entire independence of the district; the Colombian veterans, the real backbone of the liberating army, were regarded with something approaching aversion in Ecuador, and Sucre fell a victim to local animosity.

Two opposing ideas for the organization of the new states, from the territorial point of view, were early put forward. Some advocates of greater unity between these states urged that the original viceroyalties should be taken as the basis. San Martin projected a dominion which should include all the lands south of Panama; Iturbide momentarily established an empire which covered all the Spanish lands north of Panama. Bolivar himself, perhaps, went farther. The union of a very

large part of the former viceroyalties of Peru and
Nueva Granada was for a time accomplished under his
auspices. There is reason enough for believing that he
aspired to bring into the same union the rest of the
Peruvian viceroyalty and also the former territories of
the viceroyalty of La Plata. His abortive pan-American
congress was not improbably intended to be a stepping-
stone to the formation of a confederation which should
include the whole of the old Spanish empire in the
New World.

These apostles of unity, however, were not unmindful
of the localism characteristic of the race. They proposed to concede local autonomy to the provinces of
the states which they projected as local autonomy had
existed in the colonial period. Bolivar left Sucre as
his lieutenant in Bolivia; he designed to administer
Ecuador, Peru, Colombia, and Venezuela by similar
means, occupying himself the position of supreme
dictator over all the provinces; as a further concession
to local feeling, the capital was to be fixed at some place
other than one of the original capitals of the provinces.
Detesting federalism, which he characterized as 'regu-
larized anarchy', 'a law which implicitly prescribes the
necessity of dissociating and ruining the state in all its
members', Bolivar yet recognized that the immediate
union of all the Spanish American lands into a unitary
republic was impossible; he looked forward to a future
when the homogeneity of the race should be attained,
and meanwhile was content to prepare the way for a
truer union by the path of partial union. Even San
Martin, who was more frankly devoted to the idea of
an immediate coalescing of the various provinces and
who was the avowed champion of a single monarchy,
felt that the force of localism was too strong to be
overcome in a moment. After Maipú, he assented to
the practical independence of Chile under O'Higgins.

It is, perhaps, in their recognition of the impossibility

of their schemes for the moment that the truest cause of the failure of Bolivar or San Martin to carry with them the opinion of Spanish America is to be found. They were idealists who lacked faith in the practicability of their ideals; they dared not urge without qualification the adoption of the course which they felt in their hearts to be the right course. They were guilty of the blunder of recommending compromise to a race to whom compromise was antipathetic. Even had there been no other objection to their ideas, those ideas would probably have been rejected upon this ground alone. Great as the two leaders were, they yet lacked that intensity of moral courage which can impel a man to advocate that in which he believes despite all opposition, despite the seeming hopelessness of such advocacy. Not possessing such burning, such almost unreasoning faith, they were defeated from the first, defeated because to an idealistic race a non-idealistic appeal can carry no persuasion.

It may be admitted readily enough that they had good ground for their distrust of the solutions in which they believed. The vastness of the territories which they proposed to weld into a single state would have sufficed to produce the speedy dissolution of such a state even if it had been created; it would have fallen of its own weight, unless it had been maintained by the most heartfelt conviction of all its citizens. It would have fallen the more rapidly because, between its various districts, communication was so laborious. In an age when railways and telegraphs were unknown, and in a land where roads were generally little better than mule tracks, it would have been impossible for the central government to have transmitted its orders with sufficient rapidity to outlying provinces or to have dealt promptly and effectively with any distant emergency. The extreme variation of interests and conditions of life between the constituent parts of such a state would have served, moreover, to render equitable government an almost impossible task. The holders of supreme authority would in no case have possessed personal knowledge of the whole of their dominions and the measure of local autonomy which would of necessity have been conceded would infallibly have developed into independence. To the idea of such union there were also opposed local and personal ambitions, the natural jealousy existing between district and district as a result of a lack of mutual knowledge, and the equally natural rivalry between men who felt themselves to be fitted to command.

Above all, such schemes were in conflict with a tradition which had grown continually stronger in each succeeding generation of the colonial period. The *conquistadores* carried with them to the New World that sentiment of localism which had from time immemorial been prevalent in Spain, and which was so emphatically expressed even in the regnal style of the sovereigns. In America, almost everything contributed to foster that sentiment. Even had the first Spanish invaders been anything but individualists by temperament, they would have been driven to act as individualists by force of circumstances. The fact that the conquest was undertaken, not by one or two great expeditions, but by a large number of small expeditions and those private enterprises under the sanction of the crown, encouraged local feeling. That feeling was in some measure recognized and confirmed by the administrative system established by the mother country; it was in accord with physical conditions and with inevitable facts. To a conservatively minded race, the break with tradition involved by the Bourbon reforms was unpopular; that advocated by the exponents of a greater unity would have been far more unpopular because far greater, because it would have involved the acceptance of an essentially radical idea. The champions of a single state might, it is true, have argued that they were doing no more than championing the maintenance of the Spanish system, under which the authority of a single monarch had been recognized from one end of Spanish America to the other. But such a contention would have been vitiated by the fact that the seat of the government would no longer have been on the other side of the Atlantic, that it was proposed to convert a distant and nominal control into one which would have been near and actual. They were running counter to the feeling of the race and the prejudice, thus created, was not to be overcome even by the merited prestige of a Bolivar. It would not have been overcome even if the leaders had acted in accord for a common end; it was deepened by their disagreement. The somewhat mysterious conference at Guayaquil between Bolivar and San Martin suggested that the one desired an hegemony of the north and the other an hegemony of the south. It sufficed to reveal the lack of harmony between the two greatest exponents of unity, and to render more certain thereby the rejection of the type of unity advocated by either.

The rejection of the idea of a single state was also the rejection of schemes for narrower unions. Some Argentine leaders still hoped to unite with Buenos Aires the present republics of Paraguay and Uruguay; the idea of extending the newly formed republic across the Andes by the absorption of Chile was entertained, and if Bolivia had been freed by Argentine arms, its inclusion would also have been attempted. Bolivar did establish his great Colombia. But such unions were foredoomed to failure. They were not less in conflict with tradition and not less antipathetic to the conservatism of the race than were the wider schemes which had been put forward; they had the additional disadvantage of being in essence compromises. The idealism of the conception of a single state made some definite appeal; there was in it a certain magnificence which was attractive. The conception of a unity which was less complete made no such appeal; it had all the demerits of union with none of the merits; it was an imperfection. It was, indeed, certain that when the idea of one Spanish American republic or empire had been rejected, the wheel would swing full circle, and the ideal of division would replace that of union.

That it should do so was the more natural because it was in reality a conservative ideal. It was ultimately a proposal to perpetuate the administrative areas of the colonial period, during which viceregal authority over the various provinces had been little more than nominal. There was nothing radical in the suggestion that these autonomous districts should become independent republics. It was rather reactionary, a return to pre-Bourbon days, to the most truly Spanish epoch. The organizers of these new states could almost feel themselves to be the very heirs of the *conquistadores*, carving out for themselves so many quasi-independent principalities.

The acceptance of this solution was further facilitated by the existence of a number of leaders, the *caudillos*, who were all sufficiently eminent to merit high position and of whom no one was sufficiently pre-eminent to be marked out as the superior of the others. O'Higgins in Chile, Santa Cruz in Bolivia, Flores in Ecuador, Artigas in Uruguay, Yegras in Paraguay, Santander in Colombia, Paez in Venezuela, each seemed to be clearly designated for the supreme position within his particular territory, but in no sense also designated to be the heir of Bolivar or San Martin. They were the natural leaders of localism and their task seemed to be pre-ordained, the task of stereotyping the divisions which had existed from the first days of the conquest and which had been rather disguised than obliterated during the colonial period and by the prosecution of a common cause during the War of Independence.

While, however, it is true that the rejection of the idea of a wider unity was in effect the acceptance of the idea of an almost extreme subdivision, the latter was never fully realized and even its partial realization was but painfully achieved. The administrative areas of the colonial period had never been defined with complete accuracy. In a sparsely populated and partially explored country, when geographical knowledge was little exact and when trigonometrical surveys were unknown, frontiers were of necessity vaguely drawn. Those areas were also multifarious; the unit which should be selected was hence uncertain. The changes effected in the eighteenth century served to introduce a further complication; the basis of division might be sought in the Bourbon or in the Habsburg period. There was abundant cause for dispute, and the history of the period immediately following the War of Independence is largely the history of attempts to decide the area of the new republics, an attempt to decide which question was made, indeed, even before the authority of Spain had been finally extinguished on the mainland of the American continent.

Some of the questions at issue were, it is true, settled speedily enough. The wish of certain Argentine leaders to make the viceroyalty of La Plata the area of the new republic was soon found to be vain. Political union between the various constituent parts of the proposed state was never even for a moment achieved. Bolivia was liberated from the north; Paraguay asserted its freedom from Buenos Aires; Uruguay was temporarily under Brazilian control and then established its independent existence. But when a decision had been reached on these points, the political future of the remaining provinces of the present republic was still undetermined. Local feeling ran high and a considerable party desired that decentralization should be carried to its logical conclusion. The past history of the country provided an argu-

ment in favour of further division. It has been sometimes seemingly forgotten that the conquest and settlement of the territory of the present Argentine Nation,
in so far as it was accomplished at all during the colonial
period, was effected not from one direction but from
two or rather three, not from the east alone but also
from the north-west and west. Before Buenos Aires
had been finally founded, Spanish towns had been
established in the interior of the country by expeditions
which did not proceed along the rivers, but which
crossed the Andes from Peru and Chile into Tucumán
and the neighbouring districts. During the greater part
of the colonial period, San Juan, Mendoza, and San
Luis together formed the province of Cuyo which was
part of the government of Chile. Tucumán and
Córdoba were not united with Buenos Aires. The
northern districts were part of Upper Peru, were at-
tached to the *audiencia* of Charcas and were governed
from the north. Entre Rios and Misiones were ruled
from Asunción. There were thus historical grounds for
the establishment not of one republic, but of several,
and the inherent localism of the provinces was reinforced
by the influence of tradition.

The very cause which eventually decided the question
in favour of a single state, comprising all the remaining
territories of the viceroyalty of La Plata, served to post-
pone that decision for a number of years. The physical
geography of the country rendered it inevitable that
Buenos Aires should be the economic centre of the
various provinces; it was their natural door of communication with the outside world, through which
could enter the products of Europe and through which
could go forth the products of the interior. But the
fact that Buenos Aires was thus designated as the
commercial, and hence as the political, capital of the
country sufficed to excite jealousy and to arouse fear
that local independence would be destroyed. It was

certainly not without reason that the provinces suspected that they would be exploited and that the
commercial interests of Buenos Aires would avail themselves of the fortunate position of their city to create a
system which would subordinate the rest of the country
to their own profit. So strong was the dread of such an
outcome, that even the advocates of union were divided
concerning the form which the union should take; a
bitter controversy occurred between those who wished
to create a unitary and those who wished to create a
federal republic, and this controversy was complicated
by attempts to devise means by which Buenos Aires
might be controlled in the interest of all the constituent
provinces of the republic when created. The effective
result was a compromise which was really inacceptable
to both parties until the development of the Argentine
Nation exhibited the benefits of the solution reached
and until the strength of localism had been undermined
by the establishment of economic, no less than of
political, union.

The disputes by which the Argentine was long dis-
tracted were the most embittered of all those which
marked the period immediately following the gaining
of independence, but they were paralleled throughout
Spanish America. In general, the idea of division
triumphed over that of union. Bolivia detached herself from Peru; the Great Colombia of Bolivar, the
succession state to the viceroyalty of Nueva Granada,
split up into its three component parts. Both in
Colombia and Venezuela efforts were made to carry
division still further by creating a number of small
republics in place of one of greater extent. Colombia
for a time became little more than a loose alliance of
independent states; in Venezuela the compromise of
federalism was adopted. North of the Isthmus, the
same conflict occurred. Iturbide for a time converted
the old Mexican viceroyalty into an independent

empire, but Central America soon broke away, and in Mexico itself a desire for further division appeared. Texas, prior to its annexation by the United States, had a brief existence as a separate republic, and the creation of a federal system was here also found to be the only practicable method of dealing with localism. In Central America, even that method failed; the single republic was replaced by five small states, attempts to reunite which have been uniformly unsuccessful, despite common fear of North American imperialism.

Even when the process of division had been carried out to such an extent, the desire for local freedom was not wholly satisfied. In the history of the republics, a common feature has been provincial revolts, having for their object the elevation to supreme power of some one who would in the United States be described as 'a favourite son'. Superficially these risings may seem to be the product rather of personal ambition than of any other cause, but the true motive which has so frequently gathered a band of followers round a provincial leader lies somewhat deeper. Many of the supporters of the various *caudillos* have undoubtedly been attracted by the hope of themselves rising with him whom they assist to raise, but a far more potent attraction has been that afforded by the hope of seeing their own particular province secured in that position which they are impelled by their innate localism to seek for it. A special significance attaches to the fact that the majority of the leaders have been drawn from the rural rather from the urban population: they have come from the very section of the population in which local feeling is naturally at its strongest. They have believed that the freedom of their particular locality is in danger of being impaired and they have rebelled against what has appeared to them to be the domination of some other province or of a capital city.

To a great extent, this belief has been justified; the

central government has been by no means always controlled by men sincerely anxious to promote the welfare of the country as a whole and free from bias in favour of some particular district. Many of the republics are of very wide extent, and their area is relatively greater than that of any European country of the same size owing to their physical geography and to the undeveloped condition of their communications. The Spaniards, during the colonial period, constructed few roads; they were discouraged from doing so by the government to the extent that intercolonial trade was restricted. Even the famed Inca 'ways', so enthusiastically pictured by the imagination of Prescott, were little more than tracks for foot-passengers and llamas; the lack of any other beasts of burden and of all wheeled traffic rendered it unnecessary to construct anything more elaborate. The consequence was that in most of the republics, even in those of comparatively small extent, there were isolated districts and that intercourse between the seat of government and the provinces was arduous and irregular. A hundred miles in Spanish America was often equivalent to a thousand in Europe.

The result was that information concerning the conditions and interests of an outlying province, and even of provinces not far distant from the capital, was obtainable only with difficulty and when obtained was somewhat belated and also somewhat inaccurate. The exercise of direct control was hence always liable to be in actual conflict with even vital interests; from lack of knowledge and not from lack of goodwill, the central government might issue decrees prejudicial to those whom it designed to benefit. At the same time, to relinquish such direct control, to admit any wide measure of local autonomy, was fraught with danger. In view of the dominance of localism, anything which contributed to favour it was likely to develop a desire

for so great a measure of autonomy that the authority
of the central government would be reduced to a mere
shadow, even if the desire did not become one for
absolute independence. The administration of almost
every republic was thus placed in a dilemma. If it
endeavoured to rule in any real sense, it was likely
thereby to provoke provincial hostility and to excite
revolt. If it abstained from attempting to do more
than exercise a merely general control, it was likely to
be reduced to impotence and hence to arouse no less
hostility by its inefficiency. The central government
was indeed continually brought face to face with the
problem of reconciling the preservation of local freedom
with the preservation of its own effective power. It
was required to pursue the narrow path between consideration for local feeling which should not involve
the practical abnegation of its functions and maintenance of its own control which should not involve
the despotism of the capital. The solution of the
problem appeared to be so difficult as to be impossible;
its continued existence occasioned an unrest which often
culminated in revolt and revolution.

Equal difficulty was experienced in dealing with the
superficially simpler problem of reconciling individual
liberty with efficiency of government. It was not, indeed, hard to secure the freedom of the citizens so far
as that could be achieved by mere words; the rights of
man could be easily declared to be inviolable and it
was as easy to enumerate those rights in clauses of the
constitutions. Freedom of speech, freedom of the press,
equal justice, religious toleration, the right of political
association, and the rest could be and were all laid down
as matters on which there could be no debate and could
be and were asserted to be privileges with the enjoyment
of which no government might legitimately interfere.
But it was far less easy to secure that the rights, thus
guaranteed, should be also maintained, that they should

be used and not abused; nor were the efforts to do so by any means universally successful. The verbal perfection of the constitutions, indeed, was constantly in complete contrast with their imperfection in practice.

It was not for lack of entirely sincere effort to produce conformity between theory and practice. The republics were declared to be democratic in character and organization, and if the abolition of legal class distinctions and the opening of all careers to talent suffices to constitute a democratic society, such a society was constituted. The Spanish race, however, has never been democratic in the sense in which democracy is understood in such a country as England. A feature of public life in Spain has been the seeming indifference of the mass of the people to national, as opposed to local, politics; they appear to be apathetically willing to leave the conduct of the central government in the hands of a mere clique of politicians or in the hands of some individual, whether a king or another. This indifference and apathy, however, is unreal. It is the expression of a deep-seated conviction that administration is the business of those who are designed by birth, wealth, or capacity to undertake it. The Spaniard has always believed in the equality of men, but not in the equality of citizens; the humblest peasant demands and expects to receive courtesy from the mightiest grandee, but he neither expects nor desires to exercise a proportionately equal measure of political power. His democracy is and has always been local and personal.

The Spanish Americans preserved in the New World the characteristics of their ancestors in the Old; they also were democratic in the sense in which their fellows in the peninsula were democratic. The leaders of the War of Independence have sometimes been depicted as champions of democracy as understood in the United States or in England or in France; they have been represented as the disciples of Rousseau or Jefferson. They were in reality nothing of the kind. Had they been they would have failed to carry with them any considerable body of opinion, since they would have been in temper and ideas aliens. It is true enough that they used phrases which were borrowed from revolutionary France or from North America, but they used those phrases in a sense which would not have been understood by their original authors. Their conception of government was essentially Spanish; their declarations in favour of democracy were, when interpreted, only declarations in favour of the destruction of those social barriers which had been erected between the *chapetones*, on the one hand, and the creoles and *mestizos*, on the other. Birth in the Old World was no longer to be an almost necessary qualification for office.

In this they were in the fullest sympathy with those who supported them. The majority of the population of the former colonies had no desire at all to bring about the transplantation in the republics of Anglo-Saxon or French institutions; they had no wish to exchange their Spanish democracy for the democracy of any other race. The declaration that the republics were democratic did not mean that in them the people as a whole would take an active share in the central government; mere phrases in documents could not inspire them with an idea which they did not primarily entertain and which was, in fact, wholly alien from their temperament. Critics of Spanish American political life have sometimes been misled by their own conception of democracy; they have drawn an entirely false picture of peoples desiring government of the Anglo-Saxon or French type and being constantly baulked of their desire by the unscrupulous exploitation of their social inexperience by self-seeking adventurers. Superficially this picture seems to be just enough; its justness is entirely superficial. Democratic government in the

North American or European sense has not been
established in Spanish America because its establishment has not been either sought or attempted.

At the same time, the fact that the mass of the
population have not been fired by any desire of this
kind has rendered the preservation of individual liberty
more precarious or more impossible. It can hardly be
questioned that the active participation of the nation
as a whole in the direction of public affairs is a security
that the liberty of the subject will not be impaired. A
government, subjected to the jealous and vigilant
scrutiny of the people, is compelled to respect rights
which it is pledged to respect by the very terms upon
which it exists. A judiciary, of which the actions may
be freely discussed in writing and speech, will be thereby
forced to administer even justice and to refrain from
serving rather the executive power than the nation.
Those entrusted with the discharge of public functions
will tend to be less corrupt and to be more alive to their
moral obligations, if they know that they work under
the eye of a people keenly interested in the conduct of
all national affairs. Such safeguards of the liberty of
the ordinary citizen are necessarily lacking in a state,
the inhabitants of which are content to leave the conduct of the central government in the hands of those
whose business they consider it to be to conduct it.

When the republics were declared to be democratic,
it was not thereby intended that they should become,
nor did they become, democratic in the Teutonic
sense. In the same way when they were endowed with
representative institutions, it was not designed that
they should thereby be approximated to Anglo-Saxon
countries. It may at first sight appear that the congresses of those states were modelled upon that of the
United States or upon one or other of the legislative
bodies which had been created in revolutionary France.
To such an opinion some colour is lent both by the

statements of individuals and by the wording of the constitutions. The opinion is not the less fallacious. The origin of the representative bodies of the Spanish American states, and the purpose which they were most truly designed to serve, are to be sought not in England or France, but in Spain. They were not daughters of the 'Mother of Parliaments', but sons of the *cabildo abierto*.

So much becomes clear when the history of their establishment is considered. At the very beginning of the War of Independence, the inhabitants of the chief towns of each province gathered together and a *cabildo abierto* was proclaimed, the primary object of which was to resolve on the course of action to be pursued in view of the anomalous situation which had arisen in Spain. It was in most cases by these assemblies that the various juntas were established to conduct the government. It was by these assemblies that the first holders of executive power were commissioned, and it was in the *cabildo abierto* that the draft constitutions were first approved. They fulfilled approximately the same functions as those which were discharged by the Continental Congress of the English colonies in North America or by the National Assembly or the Convention in France.

The *cabildo abierto*, however, was not an entirely satisfactory medium for the ascertaining and expression of the wishes of the nation as a whole. It was a gathering of the residents in a particular locality and not of all the inhabitants of the embryo state, and it was thus more than likely that the assembly of a capital city would insensibly assume the functions of an assembly of the nation, gradually creating a tyranny of that city over the rest of the republic. Means had, therefore, to be found to secure a *cabildo* of a still wider character, and since it was an obvious physical impossibility to assemble the whole people in one spot, recourse was necessarily had to the method of representation. Here is to be found the origin of the congresses of the republics. So far as the phrases used to describe them are concerned, so far as the formal powers entrusted to them are concerned, they were borrowed or adapted from alien sources. But they were in reality intended to be an extension of the *cabildo abierto* of the Castilian municipality. The Spanish Americans during the colonial period had lived a vigorous political life in their cities and towns; they had become used to the working of local institutions and to a particular machinery of local government. They now prepared to extend those institutions to the country as a whole and to use that machinery for central government.

There is thus a clear difference in conception between the representative bodies of Spanish America and those of other lands. The *cabildo abierto* had always been a somewhat exceptional body designed to function not permanently but upon occasion; the ordinary work of administration was entrusted to those whom it selected in the first instance, the members of the *consejo*, who were not clearly responsible to it. When the *cabildo abierto* became the national congress, the original idea of its position was preserved; there was no conviction that the executive should normally be controlled by it. The relations between the president and his ministers and the congress were to be those which had existed between the *alcaldes* and *consejos* and the *cabildo abierto*. The constant assertion that the executive and legislative are distinct may be regarded as an expression of this idea; the emergency clause which appears in every constitution, and which permits the supreme power to pass legally and entirely into the hands of the head of the executive upon occasion, emphasizes the same idea. In Anglo-Saxon countries, and in those countries where political institutions have been modelled upon those of England, it is one of the principal functions of the

legislative to watch jealously over the conduct of the
executive; the acts of the latter are intended to be
constantly subjected to the criticism and supervision
of the former. In the Spanish American states, on the
contrary, the popular conception has been that when
the executive has been once established, it should be
given an almost entirely free hand; interference by the
legislative should be the exception, not the rule. In
other words the functions of an Anglo-Saxon parliament are permanent; those of a Spanish American
congress, intermittent.

This difference of conception was of obvious importance to the preservation of individual liberty,
which was in Spanish America thereby deprived of a
safeguard which it enjoys in those lands which are
endowed with Anglo-Saxon institutions. A popular
assembly, which regards the constant supervision of
the executive as its duty and its right, can be a powerful
agency for the prevention of tyranny. It will watch
over the rights of individuals and the mere knowledge
that it will so watch in itself constitutes one of the
surest guarantees against infringement of the liberty of
the subject. But a popular assembly which entertains
no such conception of its duties and its rights, which is
rather disposed to approve mechanically every act of
executive power, will necessarily be no very potent
instrument for the protection of personal freedom.
And the congresses of Spanish America were of little
or no value for the enforcement of those guarantees
which were accorded by the constitutions.

They might, perhaps, have become so if it had not
been that in all the republics there was more than a
tendency to abuse liberty, with the result that its free
enjoyment seemed to be incompatible with efficient
government. The experience of the colonial period had
hardly served to prepare the Spanish Americans for
a life of ordered freedom. They had enjoyed, during

that period, a very wide measure of liberty, but it had been an illegal liberty; it had been enjoyed not in accordance with, but in despite of law. A spirit of lawlessness was thus fostered, and that spirit was intensified by the years of revolutionary war. It can hardly be regarded as surprising that liberty so often degenerated into licence as to appear to be an obstacle to the preservation of law and order. The Spanish desire for the effective exercise of authority therefore operated to restrict individual freedom. While desiring himself to be free to do as he willed, each man was at the same time anxious that all others should be obliged to render that obedience which was due to the government; his ideal became liberty for each, but not liberty for all.

The conviction that individual freedom should be restrained was intensified by the fact that an innate turbulence of spirit, the legacy of medieval Castile, had been developed by conditions of life in the New World. Compelled to live often in almost complete isolation, in a land where they were not infrequently driven to defend themselves against hostile natives, and where the arm of justice could with difficulty reach the remoter districts, the Spanish Americans became even more individualist than the Spaniards of Spain. They were even less inclined to seek the good of the whole community, since of that community each one hardly felt that he was a member. Left to themselves, they inclined to live for themselves, and to produce a condition of entire unrest. It appeared, indeed, that the actual concession of freedom would result in perpetual anarchy, and that for the sake of preserving the social fabric from destruction, individual liberty must be abridged.

There thus developed in the case of the freedom of the citizen, the exact position which had developed in the case of local freedom. In each case there was the same difficulty in reconciling liberty with efficiency. The problem of so doing was the fundamental problem which faced the republics; their political life has been a constant attempt to discover its solution. The period since the establishment of independence has been a period of incessant striving towards the attainment of those two ideals, to attain which is the passionate desire of the race, and the attainment of which simultaneously has always seemed to be so impossible.

IX

THE SEARCH FOR EFFICIENT
GOVERNMENT

THE desire for efficient government has always been
strong in the Spanish race. It was so even during
the most turbulent periods of Castilian history; it
rendered possible the centralizing achievements of
Alfonso the Wise and it inspired the protests of suc-
cessive Cortes against the inept dalliance of a Juan II
and the still more inept dalliance of his son. It was,
perhaps, at its very strongest in the period which
saw the discovery and conquest of the New World.
By availing themselves of this desire, Ferdinand
and Isabella were enabled to consolidate monarchical
power, to reduce to obedience the nobles, to restore
order in such unruly districts as Galicia, Vizcaya, and
Estremadura, to abrogate the *fueros* and to undermine
municipal liberty. In their reign, and in those of
Charles V and Philip II, Castile showed that for the
sake of strong rule, she was prepared to part with much,
at least, of her cherished local freedom.

She showed herself equally willing for the same sake
to submit to a serious curtailment of personal liberty.
It was the desire for efficient government which rendered the reorganization of the Inquisition so universally
popular in Castile. If a love of religious orthodoxy and
a deep conviction of the truth and necessity of a rigid
Catholicism played their part, that part was still only
secondary. The *conversos* had enjoyed an immunity
from punishment which argued feebleness in the exercise of authority, and that agitation at Seville which
led Isabella to apply for the bull of inquisition was essentially a vigorous protest against the weakness of those
responsible for the extirpation of heresy. Had not the
desire for efficient government been deeply engrained
in the hearts of the Castilian people, it would have

been futile to have issued ordinances to regulate the details of private life. Ferdinand and Isabella were obeyed when they drew up such regulations, prohibiting their subjects from riding upon mules, prohibiting the use of various forms of dress and various articles of personal adornment, and in effect prescribing the proportion of income which might be legitimately expended upon luxuries. They were even obeyed when they forbade women so to veil themselves as to give added power to their magnificent eyes; 'ninguna mujer en Castilla . . . arrebozarse . . . porque (la reina) decía, que la que tal hace no es buena, é quiere hacer, ó que ya hace, traición, é ofende á su marido, é á la república.'

This desire for efficient government is not peculiar to the Spanish race, but there is a contrast between its nature in Spain and its nature elsewhere. In England and in France, the vigorous exercise of authority by the government has been desired as a means to an end; the real wish has been for the results which follow, the promotion of law and order, and the securing of the rights and liberty of the individual. Tyranny has been hated, however capable the tyrant may have been and however admittedly efficient. In Spain, efficiency has been desired as an end in itself. It has been admired for itself and not for the results which it has produced. Tyranny has been not only tolerated but popular, so long as it has been effective and unfaltering even Ferdinand VII was 'el mucho rey' until he allowed himself to be terrorized into giving way to the revolt of Riego and Quiroga. A ruler who has ruled has been by that very fact always assured of a wide measure of support, although he may have exhibited every vice save weakness.

It is in the idealism of the race that the explanation of this attitude of mind must be sought. For most men, it is almost necessary to find some tangible embodiment of an abstract ideal before that ideal can be really appreciated and to this rule Spaniards offer no exception. The admiration felt for the half-mythical figure of El Cid was admiration for him as the embodiment of the ideal of chivalry. The veneration of the Virgin has always been very largely veneration for the ideal of womanhood; the devotion which her contemporaries felt for Isabella the Catholic was devotion to her as the personification of the same ideal. In all holders of authority the Spanish have sought the same realization of the ideal; being eager to find, they have not sought in vain. It has been enough that the ruler should be firm and resolute for him to be believed to be the personification desired and for him on this ground to receive devoted support.

Those who crossed the Atlantic carried with them the qualities of their race and transmitted those qualities both to their descendants and to the natives whom they won to their own outlook upon life. During the colonial period and after the establishment of independence, the Spanish Americans eagerly desired efficient government. Realization of that ideal in the New World, however, proved to be even more difficult than it was in the mother country. For long, it could hardly have been attained even had those entrusted with authority in the various provinces been granted the fullest confidence and the widest discretion by the home government, and even had they been men of the most consummate ability. Physical conditions rendered effective action by the central power rarely possible; isolated communities had of necessity to be left very much to themselves and since the Spanish population was extremely sparse, the compelling force at the disposal of the viceroys and governors was inevitably small and inadequate.

At the same time, conditions in Spanish America tended to conspire to foster those desires which were in conflict with the desire for efficient government.

Driven very largely to provide for their own defence, the settlers retained that turbulence which had characterized their ancestors, many of whom had left Spain because in that land they found no scope for the indulgence of their riotous passions. In the New World, they engaged with impunity in illegal practices which inspired them with a certain disregard for law; they grew more impatient of control because control, when exercised at all, was exercised fitfully and with uncertain success. In a number of districts, an extraordinarily fertile soil supplied them with the prime necessities of existence without effort on their part; there was a lack of accumulated wealth and hence the penalty for resistance to constituted authority was proportionately less feared by them than it would have been by men whose laboriously gathered capital might have been endangered. In the case of the *mestizos*, the stronger Spanish strain predominated over the weaker Indian; they were as ready to be turbulent as were the most turbulent of the creoles, and perhaps more so, since under the existing order they were in a measure stigmatized from birth.

So long as the dominion of Spain endured, however, certain factors served to hold in check the turbulence of the population. Loyalty to the throne, the force of tradition, the influence of the Church, a certain sense of patriotism which led the colonists to refrain from embarrassing a government already exposed to dangerous foreign attack, all contributed to maintain a certain appearance of good order, and the conflict between the passion for liberty and that for efficiency was very largely concealed. The dissolution of the political union with Spain served to give freer rein to forces which had previously been thus restrained. All through the colonial period, a vigorous political life had existed in the various municipalities throughout Spanish America; the creoles were fully prepared to take an active part in public affairs. The opportunity to do so was now afforded them and of it they hastened to avail themselves. But their interests were local rather than national; their view of affairs was limited by experience and they were inclined to resist any attempt on the part of a central power to exert a control to which they had not previously been accustomed. It seemed to them to be wholly irrational that the proclamation of independence and the assertion of liberty should result in a curtailment of their independence and a restriction of their liberty.

It seemed to be the more irrational because in the colonial period they had been able to convince themselves of the reality of the unreal. The government of Spain had been in fact inefficient, but its inefficiency was decently veiled, and the colonists had allowed themselves to believe, more especially during the Habsburg reigns, that the solution which they desired had been attained, that they had at once enjoyed local and individual liberty and effective rule. They were, indeed, prepared to recognize that upon their freedom, restraints were imposed, but the result of such realization was merely to fill them with a stronger desire to dispense with those restraints. It was difficult to produce in their minds a willingness to subordinate local and personal considerations to national, because it was difficult to persuade them that any such subordination was necessary for the general good of the states of which they were citizens. They were not prepared to admit that efficiency of government required that there should be some sacrifice of the interests of each for the sake of the interests of all.

Such reluctance to accept restraint was intensified by the strongly individualistic spirit by which the creoles were inspired. The somewhat foolish sarcasm that Spanish American armies have usually consisted of twenty generals to each private might with more reason

be applied to the civil life of the republics; in them
there have very often seemed to be too many leaders and
too few mere followers. During the colonial period, the
creoles had been very largely excluded from any share
in the central government, but they had yet constituted
a ruling class. They had controlled the municipal affairs
of the communities of which they were members; they
had in most cases been masters of native servants. The
establishment of independence appeared to them to
involve, as a natural and legitimate consequence, that
they should enjoy a still wider authority. Each
individual felt that, if he were disposed to interest
himself in national affairs, upon those affairs he was
entitled to exercise an influence proportionate to that
which he had exercised upon local affairs. It was as if
each *alcalde* aspired to become a president, and each
regidor, each member of the municipal council, a
minister with the reversion of the presidency in store.
Each would be a *caudillo*; none could perceive any
reason why authority should be held by his neighbour
and not by himself. So far as civil experience was concerned, so far as capacity for administration was concerned, there was nothing unreasonable in the position
so adopted by the creoles. Had life during the colonial
period been really stagnant, there would have been few
enough capable of undertaking the task of government.
The activity of local political life, however, had the
effect of producing a very large number of persons, any
one of whom was almost equally fitted to assume even
the presidency of one of the new republics and every
one of whom was fully conscious of being so fitted.

The number of creole aspirants to supreme authority
was thus sufficiently great; it was increased by a very
large number of *mestizos* and even of Indian aspirants.
Under Spanish rule the inferior status of these two
classes had been recognized in fact, although not in law;
with the establishment of independence, such in-

feriority was publicly denounced, when it was explicitly asserted that the new states were democratic and that all citizens were equal. The *mestizos*, thus officially relieved of the stigma previously resting upon them, entered the field as candidates for the highest offices; they were the more eager to press their claims because not to do so might seem to indicate a willingness to submit to the reimposition of the stigma which had been removed. To a lesser degree the Indians also entered the same field. The generous enthusiasm which characterized the epoch of independence prompted declarations that the natives had been oppressed under the fallen régime and that in the new era they should regain all that of which they were said to have been unjustly deprived. So eloquent were these declarations that in Europe the war of liberation has sometimes been vaguely pictured as a war between Spaniards and Indians, the latter being supported by some few humane and liberally-minded men of the originally dominant race, despite the fact that the generals of Ferdinand VII on the whole relied far more upon native troops than did Bolivar or San Martin.

A further obstacle to the establishment of efficient government was presented by the very character of the movement which dissolved the union with Spain. That character has been greatly obscured by the actual results which followed from the War of Independence and by the fact that the leaders in the war so frequently clothed their ideas in phraseology borrowed from England or France. It has been consequently supposed that the movement was analogous to those which established the independence of the English colonies in North America or which destroyed the *ancien régime*. In actual fact, it was wholly different. The War of Independence effected a revolution but it was not designed to do anything of the kind. To adapt the somewhat hackneyed aphorism of Seeley, the Spanish Americans

established a number of republics in a fit of absence of
mind. There was no initial intention of creating a new
order; even when it had been realized that independence
was necessary and even when independence had been
achieved, the idea of clinging to the past subsisted;
that idea did not disappear even when a republican
organization for the new states had been formally
adopted. Iturbide, Bolivar, and San Martin were at
one in this, that they desired as far as might be to
preserve the old order. In this desire, they were in
accord with the majority of their supporters. The
charge brought against Iturbide was that he had attempted a revolutionary change, placing an imperial
crown on his own head instead of upon that of some
member of the royal house of Spain. Bolivar incurred
somewhat rancorous hostility not because he was a
conservative, but because he was suspected of being a
radical; not because he wished to preserve the old, but
because he was regarded as an apostle of change. The
War of Independence was the most conservative revolution which has ever occurred.

Had it not been it would have ended in failure. By
temperament, the Spanish American is and always has
been intensely conservative. He is by nature devoted
to the old; he clings to the faith of his fathers and upon
him theological modernism makes no real impression.
The mode of life which he wishes to pursue is that of
Castile and so far as he has been able to do so, he has
reproduced in the New World the atmosphere of the
Old. To him the hurry and bustle of modern life is
rootedly antipathetic; he has never been filled with
that somewhat restless activity which characterizes the
North Americans. The very passion which seems often
to rouse him is the passion of Spain, not that of New
York or Chicago; he has always cared more for beauty
than for utility, and to him the new makes no appeal by
reason of its novelty.

In politics, as in other aspects of life, the Spanish American has never been a radical or a revolutionary. It is significant of his attitude that such success as has been secured by communistic propaganda in Mexico has been due not to a wish to create a new order, but to a belief that so a return might be made to pre-conquest days by destroying the latifundia established by the heirs of the *conquistadores*. It is not less significant that the one republic where radical ideas have some hold upon the people is that into which immigration has introduced the most considerable non-Spanish element. To the establishment of efficiency this conservatism was necessarily, although unconsciously, opposed. In the past no real efficiency had been known and hence its attainment could result only from the effecting of radical changes, of a break with the old which was not desired and which was alien to the temper of the race.

The problem presented to the republics has thus always been one of extreme complexity and one of which the complexity has been increased by the idealism of the Spanish Americans. In political affairs other peoples have been content to accept a working compromise; they have forgone the full realization of their desires in order thereby to secure a solution of questions which has not been wholly satisfactory but which has been more or less practical. The Spanish Americans, however, have been impatient of anything short of perfection. They have been altogether dissatisfied with anything less than the fullest liberty; they have been altogether dissatisfied with anything less than the most complete efficiency. They have regarded with suspicious jealousy any development of the central power, as being opposed to ideal freedom. Realization that some restraint upon liberty is essential has been hindered by the conviction that any such restraint is incompatible with perfection and by the belief that in the past no such restraint was found to be requisite for the effective

working of government. At the same time, they have
been slow to realize that there should be limits to the
authority of the central power; they have inclined to
demand the completest despotism, since that also seems
to be essential to the attainment of perfection. They
have been almost constantly demanding two incompatibles, absolute liberty and absolute control. They
have hurried from extreme to extreme, finding satisfaction in neither, since the attainment of one desire
has precluded the attainment of the other. To the
colder and unidealistic temper of other races, they have
appeared to be as ants in a disturbed ant heap, furiously
running hither and thither, furiously active, achieving
nothing save the reduction of everything to a condition
of chronic unrest.

The persistent search for the ideal has led to the
emergence in every state of two parties, agreed in
desiring to attain the perfection both of liberty and of
efficiency, convinced that the perfection of each is
simultaneously attainable, but wholly at variance as
to the path which leads to the goal. The one party
holds that if liberty be assured, efficiency will necessarily
result; the other that if efficiency be assured, liberty
will thereby be secured. The one party has been ready
to sacrifice effective government on the altar of freedom;
the other to sacrifice freedom on the altar of effective
government. The one would observe to the last iota
the letter of the constitution; the other regards the
constitution as an expression of pious hopes rather than
as a practical instrument of government. Of the one
party, it may be said that it seems to regard the people
as having been made for the constitution; of the other,
that it regards the constitution as nothing but a means
to an end, to be abrogated at any moment if its preservation appears to be difficult or inadvisable. The one
party consists of believers in a pure republic; the other
of believers in dictatorship: they may be conveniently

described as republicans and monarchists, although the
latter have no wish to place a crown upon any head.

Of these two parties, the republicans have always
been the weaker, although they may with some reason
claim that their views are embodied in the clauses of
the constitutions. The party has certainly everywhere
devoted adherents; it has always possessed certain
advantages over its opponents. Its leaders have
generally been superior in oratorical talent. The
arguments which they urge are hardly to be contra-
dicted even by their opponents, so far as the theory
upon which those arguments are based is concerned.
The moral loftiness of the doctrines which they ex-
pound makes a necessary appeal to a generous race, to
which an appeal to higher considerations than those of
mere utility is never addressed wholly in vain. They
can, more readily than their opponents, defend themselves against any charge of self-seeking; they are able
more convincingly to claim to be actuated by altruistic
motives. Nevertheless, their possession of all these
advantages has rarely, if ever, sufficed to secure for
them the adhesion of more than a minority in any
state, because they have laboured also under certain
countervailing disadvantages.

Of these disadvantages, the first has been one from
which they could hardly free themselves. Almost necessarily they have expressed their ideas in phrases derived
from foreign sources, but they have gone farther than
merely to borrow words. They have repeatedly professed
to draw their inspiration not from Spain, but from
France, from England, from the United States. More
than a few of the leading republicans have been
disposed to exalt French as against Spanish culture;
some have even gone so far as to assert that all which
is most fruitful of hope for the future in Spanish
America has been received from Paris. They have at
least appeared to advocate the imitation of foreign

models, the introduction of foreign institutions, and in some extreme cases even to look for political salvation in the establishment of foreign rule; in El Salvador, they went so far as to express a desire for incorporation in the United States and to approach the state department with that object in view. They have seemed to proclaim their own race to be inferior to other races, to the French and to the Anglo-Saxons, and even to the North Americans. They have seemed to be lacking in that very faith which their advocacy of a policy which looks to the future renders so necessary to them.

The attitude which they have thus adopted is one little calculated to win a large measure of popular support. The Spanish race has always been proud, intensely nationalist and deeply patriotic. It has resented the intrusion of alien influences and has believed firmly in the excellence of its own culture and of its own institutions. To belittle that culture and to advocate the abandonment of those institutions can only be to alienate almost hopelessly the sympathies of those whose support is desired. Conscious of their possession of an old civilization, conscious of the past achievements and of the past glory of the mother country, the Spanish Americans resent the suggestion that they should learn from Paris or London or Washington. Against any such suggestion, their innate conservatism revolts; against any such suggestion they revolt not the less because they are deeply and justifiably convinced that their glory has not been dimmed for ever, because they feel assured that as the race has had a glorious past, so it is destined to have a still more glorious future, if only it has faith in itself, if only it be true to its own ideals.

The republicans, moreover, have been forced to rely rather upon theory than upon experience, since Spain has never, save for one brief and unhappy moment, been a republic and since the Spanish American states are politically youthful. But Spanish idealism has always

been marked by a realization of the practical. When
Ferdinand and Isabella set before their people the conception of a great mission to be performed, they succeeded in inspiring their subjects with an enthusiasm
hardly paralleled in the history of mankind, unless a
parallel be found in that evoked in the Saracens by
the preaching of Mohammed, an enthusiasm which
was not passing but enduring, which was proof
against disappointment and defeat when the crown had
descended to unworthy heirs and which was proof even
against the deadly canker of corrupt inefficiency and
against the biting satire of Cervantes. Ferdinand and
Isabella could never have accomplished so much had
they done no more than proclaim an ideal, had they
merely asserted that it was the mission of the race to
win the world for Christ, had they merely proclaimed
the Spaniards to be the chosen people of their God.
Their success was due to the fact that they adduced
practical illustrations of the truth of their assertions,
that they appealed to experience for proof of all that
they preached, to the lessons to be learned from the
past history of their country, to the visible signs of
divine favour supplied by the conquest of Granada and
the discovery of a New World.

The republicans could make no such appeal. On the
contrary, all the lessons of the past seemed to argue
against them. It was under the rule of her most absolute monarchs that Spain had won her greatest triumphs
and had been the foremost power in Europe and indeed
in the world. It was under absolute rule that she had
achieved the golden age of her literature and the
greatest heights of her art, that her Church had been
most flourishing and that under the inspiration of a
Spanish idealist, a Society had been founded which had
regained peoples seemingly lost for ever to the Faith
and which had carried that faith to other peoples sunk
in pagan blindness. The effort made in the early years

of the nineteenth century to create a quasi-republican order in Spain had failed; the 'Spanish Constitution' was associated not with a period of success and glory but with one of disorder and despondency, and it was easy to argue that the very grandeur of the resistance to France was attained rather in despite of, than as a result of, the existence of a liberal party in the country. Even in Spanish America itself, the greatest leaders of the War of Independence had not been champions of republicanism, one and all they had been conservative, not radical; Spanish, not French; believers in autocracy far more truly than believers in democracy.

It was, indeed, a fact that the chief protagonists of a purely republican organization of the new states were men of thought rather than of action; they were civilians, not soldiers, and their prestige was won rather in the debating hall than in the camp. Their lack of military reputation was a serious barrier to their attainment of that hold upon the popular imagination which was necessary for them if they were ever to win to their side a majority of the people. In Spain the successful soldier, and perhaps the soldier whose success has still really to be won, has always enjoyed a wide influence. Admiration for military talent, common enough among all peoples, has been peculiarly strong in Spain, very largely as a natural result of the past history of the country. That history, down at least to the end of the reign of Philip II and perhaps down even to a later date, has been correctly described as 'one long crusade'. For centuries, the outstanding feature of the political life of the peninsula was the struggle to drive out the Moors; when Granada had fallen, it became a struggle in order to secure recognition of Spanish hegemony, in order to complete the triumph of the Cross.

In Spanish America life was not less a crusade during a great part of the colonial period. The heroes of that period were fighters, not thinkers, and the race, already inclined to admire military skill above all other talent, was confirmed in that attitude of mind. The soldier in the New World had never been able to lay down his arms; in many districts, savage Indian tribes were constantly on the watch to attack and the settlers were likely to pay dearly for a single unguarded moment. Other districts were threatened by the buccaneers and by foreign assault; in others, there was a not wholly unfounded suspicion that the natives would be willing to rise, if opportunity offered, as they rose under the leadership of Tupac Amaru. At the same time, the total number of regular soldiers in the colonies was small. It was upon a militia that reliance had to be placed, and as there were relatively few Spaniards in the New World, all were perforce soldiers as long as they were able-bodied. The 'nation in arms' was a fact in Spanish America long before Von der Goltz wrote. The War of Independence naturally deepened the inclination to look for leadership to the soldier rather than to the civilian. While the war lasted it was necessary to do so; when the war was ended the heroes of the struggle exerted an inevitable predominance over those whom they had led to victory.

It might, perhaps, have been otherwise had there been in any state a civilian of such ability and of such unblemished integrity as to compel recognition of his leadership. But no such individual emerged; Bernardino Rivadavia presents only a possible exception. When independence had been established, the creoles almost immediately tended to become politicians, even if they continued to confine their attention primarily to local affairs, and for politics very many displayed a considerable aptitude. That aptitude, however, was so evenly distributed that it was no easy matter to pick out any one individual as possessed of greater capacity in this particular respect. Among the republicans there have been very many who have attained a merited reputation for oratorical ability; there have been many who have been undoubtedly sincere in their profession of the loftiest sentiments; there have been many possessed of great knowledge of the theory of government. Some test has always been needed by which their relative capacity can be gauged, and no such test has been available, save one which it has been somewhat hazardous to apply, that of entrusting power to an individual selected, as it were in the dark, from a number of possible candidates. The republicans have, in fact, paid the penalty of being rather men of thought than men of action, whereas their opponents have enjoyed the advantage of having leaders designated by practical achievement.

The republicans have been hampered also by the results which have in many cases followed upon their acquisition of control. They have sincerely endeavoured to translate their theories into facts and the consequences of this endeavour have seemed to prove the unwisdom of the ideas which they have preached. Resolved to secure local freedom, they have permitted and have even brought about an extreme of decentralization. Resolved to protect individual liberty against oppression, they have so reduced the power of the executive, that it has proved to be impossible to preserve law and order; life, limb, and property have become insecure. Under their administration, society has tended to drift into a condition of anarchy, in which even that liberty which they have so ardently championed had been at the mercy of turbulence. Their opponents have constantly been able to point to experience as proving that the pure republicans are able to secure neither efficiency nor freedom, and have themselves again and again been able to appear as the saviours of their countries. Support which the republicans might otherwise have received has been alienated from them by the disastrous results of their rule.

Even so, it is probable or certain that the balance between the two parties would have been far more nearly maintained if, as has sometimes been imagined, the republicans had possessed a monopoly of idealism. In such circumstances, they would have been the only party in harmony with the aspirations of the race. It is, however, altogether fallacious to suppose that the majority of the dictators who have arisen in Spanish America, and the majority of the followers of those dictators, have not been as sincerely idealist as any of their opponents. The contrary ideal which they have championed has been every whit as real as that of the republicans, and for this reason they have won adherents and have gained the ascendancy. They have been the apostles of efficient government, the exponents of the theory that if authority be effectively exercised, freedom will also be truly safeguarded.

In this contention, they have been in fuller accord with the majority of the population than have been their opponents. Their attitude has been essentially Spanish; if they also have adopted often an alien phraseology in which to express their ideas, they have gone no farther. They have not exalted an alien culture; they have not despised their own past. They have appeared as the inheritors of a Spanish tradition, as the true heirs of their great precursors in the Old World and in the New. The prototypes of Bolivar, of Rosas, of Francia, of Porfirio Diaz, are not to be found in England or France or the United States. These men were cast in a Spanish mould; their virtues and their faults were Spanish, and to a greater or lesser degree, they were the embodiments of a Spanish ideal.

As Spaniards they were conservative. They aimed not at the creation of a new order, but at the perpetuation and development of the old; they sought their justification in the past from which they drew their inspiration. At times, the Spanish American dictators have seemed almost consciously to have modelled themselves upon the great figures of a bygone age. Francia appears as a very reincarnation of that monarch who was to his enemies 'el demonio del Mediodía', to his admirers 'el rey santo'. The character of Philip II drawn by one Spanish historian might well stand as a character of the dictator of Paraguay: 'sombrio y pensativo, suspicaz y mañoso, . . . firme en sus convicciones, perseverante en sus propósitos y no escrupuloso en los medios de ejecución, indiferente á los placeres que disipan la atención y libre de las pasiones que distraen el ánimo, frío á la compasión, desdeñoso á la lisonja é inaccesible á la sorpresa, dueño siempre y señor de sí mismo para poder dominar á los demás, cauteloso como un jesuita, reservado como un confesor y taciturno como un cartujo, este hombre no podía ser dominado por nadie y tenía que dominar á todos; tenía que ser un rey absoluto.' Francia endeavoured to revive the regime which had existed in the former Jesuit missions; he excluded all foreigners and all foreign influences, and he held his power until his death; even after his death the Paraguayans are said to have talked in hushed whispers of 'el Difunto', not daring to utter his name. His successors in supreme power adopted a more radical policy; the younger Lopez aspired to be the Louis XIV or Napoleon of South America and plunged his country into a war so disastrous that it was crippled for generations. It is, indeed, noteworthy that those dictators have attained the greatest measure of success who have been most Spanish in their policy, who have been most really conservative. The would-be radical reformer has aroused vigorous opposition, and has generally ended his career, as did Balmaceda, as the victim of a revolution.

The dictators have gained support the more readily because they have been ready rather to lead than to attempt to drive. By that impatience of disagreement which has been so often characteristic of the radical and which is perhaps the natural outcome of his belief in the excellence of the new, the advocates of republicanism alienated those whom they attempted to convert. Propounding theses which could win acceptance only when they became familiar, and which could become familiar only by slow degrees, they have failed to recognize the necessity for patience. They have endeavoured to force, instead of endeavouring to win, confidence and they have found themselves in conflict with the temper of their race. The Spaniard has never been ready to submit to intellectual compulsion, in the sense of being ready to change his opinion at the bidding of any preacher, however eloquent. On the other hand, the monarchists were in reality advocates of the known and the familiar; the leaders of the party claimed adhesion upon grounds which had in the past supplied reason for adhesion; they might exercise despotic authority but they did so under sanctions long recognized as valid. In the majority of cases they enjoyed the advantage of military prestige; the purely civilian dictator has always been the exception. They have found in war opportunity for exhibiting their capacity for leadership; there has been available a test by which to gauge the relative ability of rival claimants to the supreme position in the state.

The very individualism of the Spanish character has also served to swell the numbers of the party supporting the monarchists. In Spanish America, as in Spain, *caciquismo* has always been present; ready admiration has been accorded to a man who in any walk of life has asserted his individuality. The dictators, whatever else they may have lacked, have never lacked personality; if they have not been notable for their virtues, they have been notable for their crimes; each one of them has been in some sense 'el mucho cacique'. Tyrants, such as the elder Lopez in Paraguay or Rosas in the

Argentine, were not ordinary men; it may be safely conjectured that in any walk of life they would have achieved notoriety, if they had not achieved fame. There have no doubt been also men of marked individuality in the republican party, but the leaders of the monarchists have found expression of their individuality more easy, if only because they have been able to seek that expression in acts rather than in words.

Above all, the monarchists have had over their opponents the advantage that they have seemingly been able to make good their promises; they have at least continually given the states which they have controlled efficient government. They have given deeds rather than words, realities rather than theories. Under their rule, anarchy has been repressed and material well-being promoted. It has been at least arguable that freedom itself has been to some extent secured, since they have maintained that general law and order without which liberty is no more than an idle word. Their supporters have been able to point to the lessons of practical experience and with some justification to allege that benefits, otherwise denied, have been enjoyed under the rule of dictators.

On the whole, they have been able to gain the adhesion of a majority of the population, but they have not been able to do more. A considerable body of hostile opinion has always existed; it has been possible to repress, but not to extinguish, opposition, and if the rule of the republicans has most frequently ended in anarchy, that of the monarchists has most frequently ended in revolution. It is only superficially just to suppose that the origin of these revolutions is to be found in the appearance of some rival candidate for equally autocratic power; if some dictators have fallen as a result of mere intrigue, the cause of the overthrow of the greater number has been something far deeper and more permanent than personal rivalries.

The régime which has been created by these men has been essentially an illegal régime. It is true that in most instances they have secured the formal sanction of some kind of popular assembly, but to pack such an assembly and to dictate its decisions has never been more difficult in Spanish America than it has been in Europe for those who wield executive power and control both the military forces and the machinery of the central government. It has never been really possible to contend that a dictatorship has been in agreement with the letter of the constitutions, save when the constitution has been revised at the bidding of the dictator; it has been far more impossible to contend that it has been in accord with the spirit of the constitutions as drafted at the foundation of the republics. The fact that after the event a revolution has been approved counts for nothing. It is merely idle to suggest that a dictator, installed in power by the arms of his followers or as a result of successful intrigue, has been genuinely prepared to submit the question of his continuance in power to the free and unfettered judgement of the citizens. Popular votes given in his favour mean as much and as little as did those *plébiscites* which were the favourite device of Napoleon III. The illegality in their position has been prejudicial to the dictators, who while professedly conservative in their attitude, have been actually driven to radicalism. They have proclaimed themselves to be the saviours of a dissolving society; they have professed to be the champions of an order threatened with destruction by those who would break away from the past. At the same time, they have been compelled to override the fundamental laws of their states and in fact, if not in theory, to introduce violent changes in the organization of the republics under their control. This inconsistency has not escaped the notice of the Spanish Americans and it has afforded a convenient basis for attack upon the monarchists; the republicans have been able to assume the position of guardians of established institutions.

Imperfection of communications has also presented an obstacle to the peaceful continuance of a dictatorship. It has resulted in the continual occurrence of revolutionary interludes. In a frankly monarchical state, and more especially in a state definitely organized upon an autocratic basis, the holder of supreme power may with some profit to himself remain personally unknown even by sight to those over whom he rules. Diocletian, hidden in the palace of Nicomedia, Philip II, buried in the recesses of the Escorial, probably wielded all the greater power by reason of their very seclusion; they became invested with a double measure of that mystery which surrounds a monarch and it was the more easy for them to inspire their subjects with a species of superstitious awe. They were able also to enhance the respect felt for their quasi-divine position by being careful to show themselves in public only in circumstances calculated to provoke wondering admiration; when they did appear, it was surrounded with all the pomp of majesty.

But the autocratic ruler of a theoretically democratic state is in a very different position. His authority is professedly based not upon divine right, but upon popular will. Ostensibly he is no more than the first citizen of the republic and any assumption on his part of a regal position immediately tends to expose the inconsistency of his practice with his professions. He is driven to court popularity; his tenure of power will be most secure if his subjects can feel not that he is some mysterious being exalted far above them, but one of themselves marked out for eminence only by reason of his greater capacity. It is vital to him that those whom he rules should be able to convince themselves that they are ruled of their own free choice by one whom they know and whom, because they know, they have also selected to be their governor.

In Spanish America, however, difficulty of communication made it inevitable that the dictator should
be a stranger to the majority of the inhabitants. Except
within a comparatively small area, he has been no more
than a name or the symbol of a vague power, the intervention of which has been more often resented than
welcomed. If by some he has been regarded as the
embodiment of that which they have approved in the
constitution, by many more he has been regarded as
the embodiment of that which they have disapproved.
The dictators have in fact been constantly prevented
by the very extent of their states from securing that
personal devotion which has always been the most
valuable asset for any one ruling over Spaniards. This
has been the greater disadvantage to them since it has
rendered far more difficult the task of meeting possible
rivals and has at the same time rendered the emergence
of rivals more probable and easy. The very isolation of
the various provinces in each republic has facilitated
the rise in them of *caudillos*, who have been able to
attract to themselves a following as numerous as that
which has adhered to the dictator for the time being.
In their own immediate area, these leaders have secured
a more or less undisputed control and that with little
difficulty. The growth of their power has been concealed by distance. It has sometimes been aided by the
central government itself, compelled by difficulty of
communication to delegate authority to some local
governor. It has been allowed to develop, even when
its existence has been known and feared, because its
development could be checked only by the employment of armed force, a difficult and hazardous method.
Local influence, thus gained, has served to fire the
ambition of its possessors. Supreme in their own
districts, the *caudillos* have been tempted to dream
of a wider supremacy and to bid for the control of the
entire state. Every dictator has thus been brought face

to face with the danger of a sudden attack upon his position from some more or less distant province; the majority of successful revolutions have been led by men whose strength has lain in local support and who in the obscurity of a remote province have gathered the force necessary to overthrow the central government.

The danger to any dictatorship has been increased by the localism of the race. There has always been a tendency for each province to believe, whether with or without justification, that its interests are being sacrificed to those of some other province, and more especially to those of the district in which the central government has its seat or to those of the district from which the dictator has come. Each province has felt that its natives have not received their due share of preferment; that in the distribution of taxation undue burdens have been laid upon it; that the allocation of expenditure for public works has been unfair to it. The very eagerness of many of the dictators to promote material prosperity has often contributed to increase their difficulties by intensifying local opposition to them. There is no district in any Spanish American republic which can be said to be developed to its fullest capacity, with the possible exception of some small part of the Argentine. It is, however, an obvious impossibility for the government of any state to develop all parts of its territory equally and simultaneously; even were the necessary capital available the necessary labour would be lacking. Whatever is done to increase material prosperity, there is thus bound to be some dissatisfaction; some province will feel that it has been neglected and will be roused to hostility towards the central government. So alive have some of the dictators been to this danger, that they have attempted the impossible. They have initiated schemes involving an expenditure which their states have been unable to bear; they have contracted foreign loans, the amount of which has been unjustified by the actual economic condition of their states; they have granted to foreign capitalists lavish concessions which have even threatened to impair national independence and to undermine national security.

Into such mistakes, which have afforded opportunities to their opponents and which have increased hostility towards them, even the best-intentioned of the dictators have fallen. But the dictators have not been all well-intentioned. They have varied greatly in character, almost from the extreme of benevolence to the extreme of malevolence. Some have been so intoxicated with power as to lose all sense of proportion. Rosas defied the combined forces of France and England; Francisco Lopez dreamed of a Paraguayan hegemony over South America; Castro was seemingly prepared to challenge the powers to combat. Even many of those who have been more temperate have fallen very far short of perfection. They have, at the best, failed to appreciate the arrival of the hour when they could no longer profitably serve their countries. Porfirio Diaz might have ended his reign in glory had he not clung to power which he was no longer capable of wielding, and his case was that of many others. They have displayed an impatience of even friendly criticism and of even the mildest opposition which has led them to adopt a course of action calculated to arouse bitter hostility. Balmaceda, inspired by high ideals, came into violent conflict with the Catholic Church and with the Chilean congress; his attempt to override opposition produced a civil war, and a great career was ended by suicide. The dictators have, in fact, continually suffered from a common defect of idealists; they have been too ready to make haste to do good; they have had in fullest measure the defects of their qualities.

All these factors have served to strengthen opposition to such quasi-monarchical régimes, but the factor which more than any other has served to produce reaction against the dictatorships has been the failure of the dictators to realize both the ideals of the race. They have generally secured a considerable measure of efficiency and have given their states periods of good order; they have generally enforced the law as between private individuals, even when they have overridden the law in the interests of the executive. They have, however, done this at the cost of an undoubted curtailment of liberty. In the more extreme cases they have established a veritable tyranny over the private lives of the citizens. Francia created so complete a reign of terror that men dared only speak in hushed voices of 'el Supremo'. Estrada Cabrera in Guatemala was credited with delaying the operation of the postal services, while he read and censored the private correspondence of all those resident in the republic; he is said to have complained to the representative of a foreign power that the diplomat's handwriting was illegible and to have shown a revealing knowledge of his family affairs. In almost every case the press has been shackled and free expression of opinion denied. The guarantees provided for the freedom of the man and of the citizen have been in effect abrogated. Justice has been subordinated to political considerations; offences, unknown to the law, have been arbitrarily created; punishments, forbidden by the law, have been inflicted; private property has not been secure against usurpation by the executive.

But while the methods of very many of the dictators have repressed liberty, those methods have altogether failed to root out an innate desire. Nothing has sufficed to extinguish the love of freedom in the hearts of the Spanish Americans; the race has held to its ideals despite all. Persecution has, indeed, perhaps served to foster devotion to the persecuted cause; in the republics, as in the early days of Christianity, the blood of the martyrs has been the seed of the faith. With every act of oppression, the feeling of hostility to the oppressor has grown and that hostility has sooner or later found expression in action. The people have risen in defence of the ideal of local and individual liberty and have overthrown the dictatorship.

It has been the case, indeed, that the failure of the dictators to satisfy the love of liberty has been more and more dangerous to the continuance of their power with every year that they have reigned. In all lands political memories are proverbially short; past benefits are far less vivid in the minds of a people than present evils. In Spanish America the existence of a high idealism has served to produce an even more ready forgetfulness of good received than elsewhere. In their inception the dictatorships have been generally welcomed as bringing anarchy to an end; the dictator has been acclaimed as the saviour of society and as the exponent of the ideal of efficient government. Men have been ready to forgo something of the liberty which they prize for the sake of the efficiency which they prize no less; their very idealism has momentarily reconciled them to an almost inordinate extension of executive power. But when the dictator has achieved the immediate purpose which he has been created to achieve, a reaction almost immediately begins. It is as if the political consciences of the people had been stunned by the prevalence of anarchy and revive as soon as anarchy is ended. The longing for freedom becomes constantly stronger; the memory of the disastrous consequences of past attempts to satisfy that longing fades, and with it the memory also of the practical benefits which had resulted from the rule of a dictator. The conflict of the two parties is resumed; the search for the simultaneous realization of the two ideals is once more vigorously prosecuted.

The monarchical régimes which have been created again and again have in fact failed no less than the republican régimes to supply a solution of the ultimate problem. They have not attained at once efficiency and freedom, and hence they have not produced content. Intensity of political feeling has remained and has produced an atmosphere of restlessness which has to foreign observers often seemed to be perpetual revolution. The political history of Spanish America has appeared to many to be a fruitless contest between warring factions, a mere struggling of turbulent fools or self-seeking knaves.

Had the Spanish Americans been in fact a race either of fools or of knaves, it may be reasonably supposed that their political history would have been far less tempestuous. Were they fools in politics they could be deceived, were they knaves they could be bribed, into acquiescence with an established order, however imperfect and perhaps however corrupt. It is because they are neither knaves nor fools that they have not been led so to acquiesce, because on the contrary they are idealists and because it is only through toil and tribulation that an ideal can ever be attained, if it be attainable at all. Of their idealism they have given abundant proof, by their generous and whole-hearted admiration for that which is the best. Nowhere was the conception of the League of Nations so cordially received, nowhere was it so genuinely welcomed and supported, as in Spanish America, and it is the merest cynicism to suppose that the support of the republics was merely accorded because the United States abstained from giving such support. It was the idealism of the race which primarily determined its attitude. Since the creation of the League of Nations, the enthusiasm of Spanish America for it may seem to have somewhat cooled; the impression that it has done so is undoubtedly a true impression. It has been cynically suggested that the ardour of the republics did not extend to the making of any pecuniary sacrifice. It is a far more probable suggestion that the cause of a decline of enthusiasm is to be sought not in America but in Europe, that it is the failure of the League of Nations to justify the expectations formed which has lost for it the favour of a race, itself ready to cling to the ideal through good report and ill, itself full of that faith which it finds to be so wanting at Geneva.

Belief in the ideal and faith are the factors which determine the attitude of Spanish Americans towards all political questions. They believe in the attainability of perfection and they will be content with nothing less than the perfect. They have faith in themselves and in their future, a faith which has been proof against all the disappointments and all the disillusionment of the period of independence. Because they have this faith, they are content with no régime which does not give them both the maximum of liberty and the maximum of efficiency. They believe both to be simultaneously attainable and they continue to face the problem of such attainment sincerely, convinced in their own minds that its solution will be reached.

For this conviction they may seem to have no reason. It may appear that the liberty which they desire is nothing but anarchy, the efficiency nothing but despotism. It may appear that the teaching of the past history of all lands shows that in this imperfect world men must be content with something less than the ideal. It may appear that their hope is folly and their faith vain. But to their conviction, to their hope and to their faith, the Spanish Americans must hold almost whether they will or no. For it is born of that political idealism which is inherent in the race.

X

THE FUTURE OF SPANISH AMERICA

THE difficulty of the problem confronting the Spanish Americans may be gathered from the fact that nowhere in the world has a solution which would satisfy the aspirations of the race been reached. Nowhere have the ideals of efficiency and liberty been simultaneously realized. It is the pride of Englishmen to believe that in England perfection of state organization has been most nearly secured. They can with justice point to that immunity from violent change which their land has so long enjoyed, to the fact that their peculiar institutions have been imitated the world over and that these imitated institutions have worked most smoothly when they have most closely conformed to their originals. But to the Spanish mind the English system falls far short of the ideal. Government does not appear to be really efficient; in a time of acute national crisis it can only with great difficulty and at best incompletely compel all citizens to serve the state; it cannot prevent the public exhibition of a cinema film of which it declares its disapproval. The people do not appear to be in enjoyment of real liberty, for they are hedged about with restrictions; they may not even drink what they please when they please in public restaurants; they may not purchase cigarettes after a certain prescribed hour except from automatic machines. To every existing system of state organization, similar objections might be raised; all, when subjected to the Spanish test, are imperfect, since no one achieves the realization of the two ideals. So true is this that it may appear that the problem has not been solved because it is insoluble, because man is imperfect and all human institutions must partake of the nature of man.

This somewhat melancholy conclusion may be abundantly justified by experience and may be in actual fact the true conclusion. It is, however, one which the Spanish Americans have never been prepared to accept. They have always believed in the practicability of the ideal in every relation of life, and this belief has not been shaken because it may seem to be hopelessly in disaccord with realities. It has made no difference to their conviction that the ideal in love has perhaps never been attained, or the ideal in literary composition, in painting, in sculpture, in oratory. It has made no difference that even the greatest saint has been something of a sinner, the greatest general something less than invincible, the greatest hero something unheroic. Don Quixote still remains the type, and the windmills are still giants, and Aldonza is still Dulcinea. The race has not less continued to believe in the practicability of the ideal in politics. Were that belief less firm, despair would take the place of hope; every attempt to organize society would be abandoned, since nothing less than perfection deserves the effort of attainment. But Spanish faith is enduring as well as strong, and so the search for the ideal continues, so anything less than the ideal remains unacceptable. So it will be until either victory be gained or the temper of the race be changed.

To very many foreigners, convinced that the ideal is in truth unattainable, it has appeared that it is in the prospect of a change of temper that the fairest ground for hope is to be discovered. To this view some Spanish Americans have themselves subscribed; they have in effect contended that their political problem can only be solved by abandoning all attempts to solve it. It has been argued that the Spanish conception of the political ideal is radically false, that it is inconsistent with well-ascertained facts and that it should therefore be rejected. The unwillingness of the Spaniards to learn from non-Spanish peoples has been condemned. The race has been urged to rid itself of its pride, to free itself from intellectual isolation, to adopt foreign ideas and deliberately to copy foreign models.

In other lands such Spanish Americans have been hailed as prophets of the real, as being alone sensible of those defects in their fellows which present so fatal an obstacle to progress. It is by no means uncommon to find in North American writers the suggestion that the Spanish Americans can have no hope of advance, that they must remain for ever backward and inferior, unless they modify their whole outlook upon life. They are earnestly advised to adopt the business methods and the commercial ideas of the United States. They are equally advised to imitate the political practice of that great republic. They are recommended to go to school at New York or Washington, to enter, as it were, a North American correspondence college and to remember that for the present they can aspire only to a lowly position in the bottom class.

Such advice may conceivably be altogether salutary; it is certain enough that, whether salutary or not, it will not be followed. Those who tender it forget that they are addressing themselves to a proud and to an imperial race. They forget that the Spanish Americans are possessors of a culture which was centuries old before the United States came into existence, which is, indeed, older than that of the lands whence came the first rude settlers of the original thirteen states of the Union. An exhortation to a Spaniard that he should endeavour to profit from the experience and example of the North Americans seems to him to whom it is addressed to be equivalent to a similar invitation addressed by some callow undergraduate to a retired ambassador. It appears to be not less impertinent and to merit not less contemptuous treatment. The fact that the United States has attained almost unparalleled material prosperity, and that it may be in some sense almost in the position of a world arbiter, makes no essential difference. The contempt felt is not the less intense because it may be necessary to conceal it; the advice is no more regarded because it is given by those who are possessed of the capital so urgently needed for the development of the republics. The Spanish American feels no inclination to abandon his traditional outlook upon life. He has no wish to adopt those criteria of conduct which are accepted in North America; he will not voluntarily exchange his idealism for materialism. Present misfortunes do not lead him to forget the glories of the past; they rather impel him to evoke memories of those glories, to win hope from the reflection that what has been may always once more be. He is rather confirmed in his faith; he becomes more than ever convinced that, if only he believes, 'all things are possible to him that believeth,' that if only he be true to himself, if only he preserve his individuality, he will attain the fulfilment of every desire and of every hope.

The suggestion that by abandoning their traditional, and by adopting a new, outlook upon affairs, the Spanish Americans can find political salvation, betrays indeed a misunderstanding of the temper of the race. A like misunderstanding of past history and of the fundamental character of the republics is betrayed by another suggestion which has been sometimes urged. It has been argued that the existing political condition of the republics is the result of inexperience and that the remedy for that condition will be found as soon as the necessary experience has been gained, as soon as the institutions which have been created function in a real sense. At the root of this suggestion there lie two misapprehensions. It is based on the wholly erroneous assumption that, prior to the War of Independence, the Spanish Americans knew nothing of self-government. Such a supposition exhibits an entire failure to appreciate the very vigorous municipal life of the colonial

period. It involves a misreading of history, analogous
to that which would regard the Tudor period as barren
of constitutional interest and as having witnessed no
constitutional progress, because for all practical purposes parliament registered the will of the crown and
because the Commons readily assented to the most
unreasonable and arbitrary demands of Henry VIII.
The suggestion is further based upon a second and equally
erroneous supposition, the almost inevitable corollary
of the first. It has been held that the institutions, with
which the republics have been equipped, were borrowed
from England or France or the United States. This
contention is supported by reference to the terms of
the constitutions and to the outward form of the
various assemblies, but it is not the less due to a misconception of the underlying spirit of the organization
of the republics and of their historical development.
It neglects the fact that the modern congress in these
states is really an evolution of the *cabildo abierto*, and
that the effort is not to impose institutions of foreign
origin, but to apply to the central government the
principles and the machinery of Spanish local government. In knowledge of these principles and in the
working of that machinery the Spanish Americans
have no lack of experience; they have no need to
familiarize themselves with the unfamiliar since they
have no wish to achieve the organization of their states
upon alien models. They are no more inclined to go
to school in England than they are to go to school in
the United States; their conception of representative
government is not Anglo-Saxon, but Spanish. Any
suggestion that their way of salvation lies in conforming
themselves to English ideas is as fatuous as the suggestion
that they should acquire the North American view
of life.

Nor is there more justification for the further suggestion that their political salvation depends upon the

disappearance of *caciquismo*. It has been argued that everywhere there is an inordinate readiness to follow some individual and that this readiness prevents the evolution of true democracy in the republics. The first necessity of Spanish America is declared to be that the inhabitants of these states should learn to consider rather principles than persons, to cure themselves of their admiration for leaders and more especially of their admiration for military leaders. The appearance of dictators would thus become impossible; the constitutions would come into operation; government would become democratic, and unrest would end.

Such a suggestion would be reasonable enough were it not that it is based upon an entire misunderstanding of the situation. It imagines that the Spanish Americans desire to establish democratic states on the European or North American model and that they are restless because such states have not come into being; it imagines that dictators have secured power contrary to the will of the majority of the citizens or by gaining an unmerited degree of support upon purely personal grounds. It forgets that the Spanish Americans are concerned only to find a means to an end and that the principles to which they are devoted are something far higher than the principle of representation or the principle of democracy. It forgets that since it is of this end that they are always thinking, to them the means are of minor importance; that they care little whether the means be democratic or autocratic, and that if they have a preference, it is rather for a monarchical than for a republican system. It may be that *caciquismo* is an evil; even so, the removal of this evil would not end the conflict since it would not solve the problem.

The Spanish American republics must, in fact, find their own solution for a problem which is peculiarly their own, and if it is to be found at all, it can only be by keeping steadfastly before them their ideals and by

continuing to strive for their attainment. It is not by
a change of outlook that they can win salvation. For
the race to adopt any other point of view than the
Spanish would be morally disastrous. It is not that
another point of view is necessarily inferior; it is still
less that other nations should conform to the Spanish
idea of life. It is that for the Spaniard to change his
outlook would mean the abandonment of an idealism
which is innate in him and for which it would not
be possible to find a substitute, since an acquired
idealism must necessarily be very largely fictitious and
can never have the force or afford the inspiration of one
which is part and parcel of the very nature of a man.
A change of outlook would involve deterioration; it
would leave the race barren of real faith; it would mean
that the race had become false to its conception of its
duty and of its destiny. At present the Spanish
Americans strive towards a goal, well worthy of attainment; it may be in reality a matter of secondary importance whether the goal be in fact attainable, since
for a race, no less than for an individual, it is perhaps
true that 'it is better to travel hopefully than to arrive'.

To the pessimist and to the cynic, the goal sought is
indeed unattainable. It would be indeed a new experience for man were anything human to achieve perfection. Nor can it be said that the ideal has been even
nearly reached in any Spanish American state; nowhere
has the perfection of liberty and efficiency been simultaneously secured, and it may with some justice be
contended that in the majority of the republics, nothing
approaching the perfection of either has been attained.
Nevertheless, towards the solution, not of the problem
as a whole, but of a part of the problem, considerable
advance has been made. To a great extent patient and
ordered search for the solution has replaced restless
striving, and that without any sacrifice of ideals and
without any change of mental attitude. The conflict

of parties has in the past been violent and unrestrained; it has been marked by recurring revolutions, by the invocation of armed force, by proscriptions, by punishments, by judicial murders, by assassinations, by confiscations. In some of the republics it is still so marked; in others it is so no longer, and in these states, while neither party has abandoned its principles, both have agreed to endeavour to secure the triumph of their views by legitimate means. There has been a very notable advance towards stability; the constitutions have been observed in place of being infringed; they have come to represent facts instead of being little better than mere verbiage, so many sad memorials of beautiful theories wholly out of accord with actualities.

In those republics, where this change has occurred, certain features appear. In them, certain changes have been effected which may legitimately be regarded as having rendered the advance which has been made a possibility. The Argentine is to-day one of the most stable and well-ordered states not only in America but in the world; it is one in which revolution is as improbable as it is in England. But in the early years of its independent existence, it was the scene of the most bitter and violent conflict; the quarrels of the federalists and the unitarians were even more acute than were the quarrels of parties in other states. The cessation of strife ensued upon two developments, the rapid increase of population as a result of the encouragement of immigration and the improvement of communications by the building of an extensive network of railways. Uruguay was the scene of conflict between the Blancos and the Colorados and was the prey of constant civil war. Here again the growth of population and the improvement of communications has been followed by the attainment of political stability. Until a comparatively recent date Venezuela was regarded as a backward state and was in a constant condition of unrest, from which it was hardly delivered by a succession of dictators. The country has enjoyed a long period of tranquillity; the various districts of the republic are being rapidly linked together by a system of motor roads and railways and every effort is being made to encourage the necessary immigration. Rapid progress has taken the place of stagnation.

The moral of these facts is so obvious that it need hardly be pointed. The most fruitful cause, not indeed of strife between parties which is the result of a vigorous political sense and of an ardent pursuit of ideals, but of disordered conflict, is to be found in the spirit of localism. Districts isolated from one another are mutually hostile and jealous; districts isolated from the seat of government are always ready to suspect that their interests are ignored. The development of communications supplies an obvious remedy against excessive localism by bringing the various provinces into touch with one another and with the central power and by promoting an interchange of population. The isolation of individuals is a further cause of violence of conflict. Men who are compelled to live almost apart from their fellows and who are obliged to fend for themselves, have neither the occasion nor the inclination to consider their duty to society as a whole, since of society they hardly feel themselves to be members. In any sparsely populated country such cases of isolation must necessarily be common, cases of men filled with a burning love of individual liberty which becomes irrational and which borders upon love of unrestrained turbulence. The growth of population brings each into closer contact with his fellows. It serves to induce a more ordered love of freedom by creating new ties and by promoting a sense of interdependence, a spirit of co-operation and a conviction of community of interest.

Roads, railways, and increased population serve the

more to produce a calmer pursuit of the ideal because
they lead naturally to enhanced material prosperity.
From the earliest days of Spanish rule down to the present
moment the great needs of Spanish America have been
an improved labour supply and improved communications. These needs were realized by the settlers who resisted the 'New Laws' and who blazed the trail through
virgin forests, across swamps and over mountains, in
order to open ways from one province to another.
The importance of abundant labour was appreciated
by Ferdinand and Isabella, who granted a free passage
to the Indies to agriculturists and artisans; it was even
appreciated by Las Casas, who, if he would have exempted the Indians from toil, was yet ready to seek for
some other source of supply. The necessity for improved communications was felt by Charles V, who
ordered the survey of a canal across the Isthmus and
who was eager to find means by which the vast river
system of South America might be utilized to the full.
But neither need has ever been satisfied. To-day there
is not a Spanish American republic which would be
unable to support with advantage an infinitely larger
population or in which the limit of development of
communications has been even nearly reached, great
as the advance in the latter direction in the Argentine
and in Uruguay has been. That degree of material
prosperity which might be enjoyed is hence not enjoyed;
the natural resources of the various states are still
largely untapped and their potentialities are very far
from being realized. Every approach towards fuller
economic development serves to curb that spirit of
unrest which is natural to those who have little to
lose from restlessness. Increased prosperity with the
resultant increase of capital can but make for greater
calm. The race will continue to seek a solution of its
political problem, but it will be sought less tempestu-
ously, although not less sincerely.

It is by such means that the Spanish American
republics may advance towards their goal. It is no
question of imitating foreign methods of government.
It is a matter of very secondary importance whether
their government assumes an autocratic or a democratic
form, and it is, perhaps, only Anglo-Saxon vanity which
supposes that the institutions created by the English
race are those best suited to secure the true development of all nations. Government is, after all, no more
than a means to an end; that form is alone desirable
which serves the end. By the Spanish Americans this
truth is profoundly realized; to them, more than to
any other race, the method is far less important than
the results of administration. Their fervent desire is
for efficiency coupled with liberty. They seek an ideal
which is their own, the ideal of efficiency as they understand it and the ideal of liberty as they understand it.
Because the ideal is their own, the method of attainment must also be their own; it cannot be learned from
any other people, since by no other people is the same
ideal sought. They can reach their goal only by their
own road.

Whether that goal will ever be reached, whether
the road can be found, it is impossible to say. If
success be gained, the achievement will be one more
glorious than any in the annals of mankind. It will prove
that the perfectibility of man is no idle dream, that a
perfect human institution is no mere illusion. Even if
success be never gained the present is yet magnificent
and the future bright. To those who have eyes to see,
there is to-day presented the spectacle of a race
striving whole-heartedly towards the realization of its
ideals, of a race content with nothing less than the
best. In the future this spectacle will be equally
presented. The Spanish Americans are set upon a
course, from following which they will not be deterred
either by the obstacles which they find set in their

way or by the scornful incredulity of other nations. As they have been, so they will be, true to themselves. For in them burns that faith which in the past carried the crusade against the Moors to a triumphant conclusion, which made possible the conquest and civilization of vast lands by a mere handful of men, which has in these last days created a number of flourishing and progressive states. By a race, so inspired, all may be achieved in the future; its faith is that which can remove mountains, and to those who possess it, nothing can be declared to be impossible.